Accessory *CHIC*

Accessory CHIC

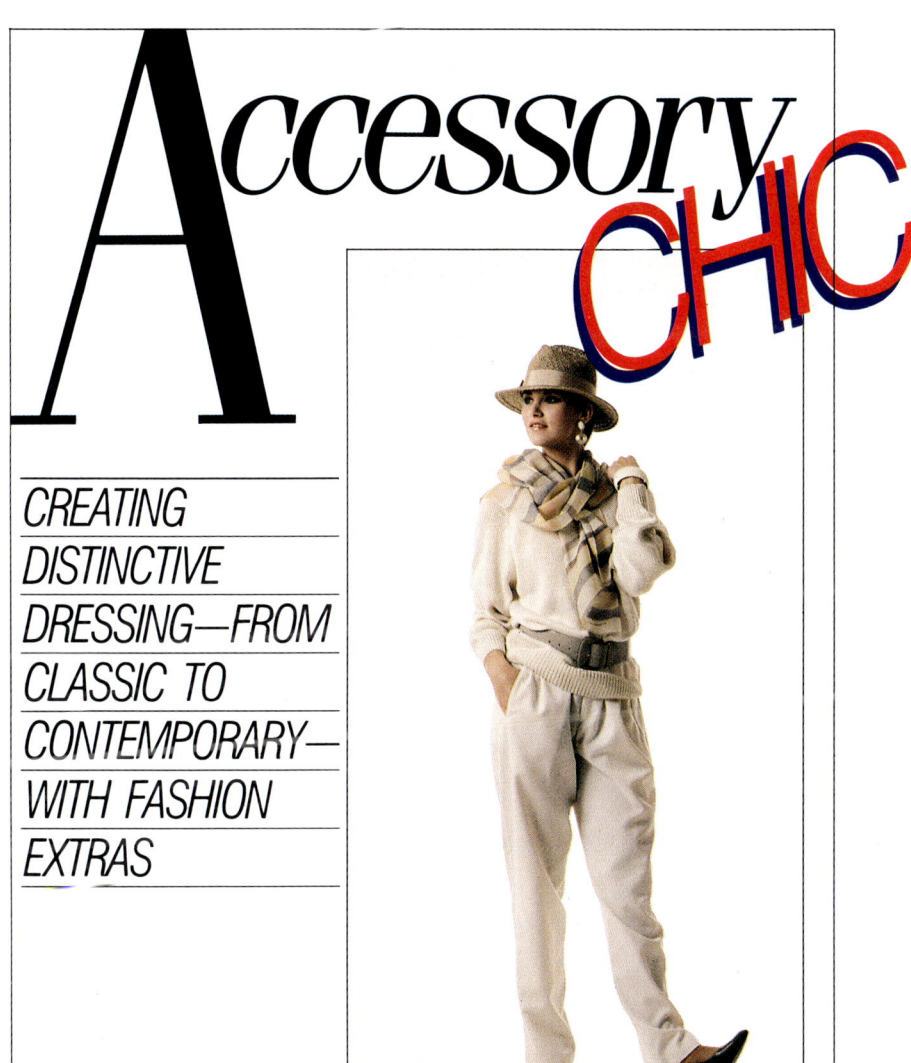

CREATING
DISTINCTIVE
DRESSING—FROM
CLASSIC TO
CONTEMPORARY—
WITH FASHION
EXTRAS

KYLE RODERICK

WINDWARD

A QUARTO BOOK

Copyright © 1986 by Quarto Marketing Ltd.
All rights reserved under the Pan-American and International
Copyright Conventions. No part of this publication may be
reproduced, stored in a retrieval system, or transmitted, in
any form or by any means, electronic, mechanical, photocopying,
recording or otherwise, without the prior written permission of
the copyright owner.

Windward
an imprint owned by WH Smith & Son Limited
Registered No 237811 England
Trading as WHS Distributors,
St. John's House, East Street, Leicester, LE1 6NE
ISBN: 0-7112-0441-1

*ACCESSORY CHIC: Creating Distinctive Dressing—From Classic
to Contemporary—with Fashion Extras*
was prepared and produced by
Quarto Marketing Ltd.
15 West 26th Street
New York, New York 10010

Editor: Karla Olson
Designer: Rod Gonzalez
Photo Researcher: Susan M. Duane
Production Manager: Karen L. Greenberg

Typeset by BPE Graphics, Inc.
Colour separations by South Seas (Far East) Graphic Art Company
Printed and bound in Hong Kong by Leefung-Asco Printers Ltd.

ACKNOWLEDGMENTS

First of all, I must thank my editor, Karla Olson, for her enthusiasm, humor, wise counsel, and sharp editing. Marta Hallett, Susan Duane, and Louise Quayle also gave me invaluable help during the production of this book. The other people I owe thanks to are: Naomi Black, Russell Bryant of *Tony Bryant Designs*, Jane Saks and Pat Roscio of *Liz Claiborne Accessories*, Ilene Kaufman, Lisa Maria Radano, Dan Koeppel, Bob Mirales, Steve Savage, Michael Pollack, Howard Lagoze, Jane Paulk, Larry Mandel, Doug Hoffman, Monique Potel and Jim Martin of *Paris Style Creations*, Michelle Diamant, Jane Jansen Seymour, Anne Soorikian Bonadies, Andrea Soorikian, Carol Motty, Linda Nathanson, Keni Valenti, Maria Martinez, Lou Stathis, Stuart Cohn, Sarah Bloomer, Beth Rubino, Richard Bowditch, Peter Landon, and Michael Montes.

CONTENTS

INTRODUCTION
THE BASIC WARDROBE
Page 8

CHAPTER ONE
FOCUS ON EYEWEAR
Page 16

CHAPTER TWO
LEGWEAR AND LINGERIE
Page 28

CHAPTER THREE
JEWELLERY
Page 50

CHAPTER FOUR
FOR YOUR FEET
Page 72

CHAPTER FIVE
ON THE TOP
Page 88

CHAPTER SIX
SATCHEL STYLE
Page 102

CHAPTER SEVEN
WRAPPING IT UP
Page 112

CHAPTER EIGHT
DRESSING RIGHT FOR DAY AND NIGHT
Page 128

APPENDIX ONE
GLOSSARY
Page 148

APPENDIX TWO
A SHOPPER'S GUIDE AND SOURCES
Page 151

INDEX
Page 154

THE BASIC WARDROBE

INTRODUCTION:

Today, more than at any other time in fashion history, women have the freedom, imagination, and resources to achieve a level of personal style that is both elegant and appropriate for work, leisure, or sport. All that is needed is a basic wardrobe with various thoughtfully chosen accessories for each outfit. The basic concept of *Accessory Chic* is to assemble a wardrobe that, through skillful coordination of accessories, is greater than the sum of its parts. Although some accessories may pose a considerable financial proposition, their long-term value to wardrobe and lifestyle is well worth the investment.

If an expensive water buffalo briefcase is guaranteed not to show signs of wear for ten years, then you will be making a very sensible addition to your wardrobe—not to mention your career. If you are hesitant to invest in a pair of diamond stud earrings, remember that they will last forever, they're perfect for both office and evening wear—and maybe someday they'll become a family heirloom!

Accessories pull the perfect look together by accenting your clothing and giving your outfit greater visual impact. They also help you get more for your money. With accessories you can alter an outfit to suit every occasion—enhancing different elements of its design with colour, texture, and shape. For example, you can turn a conservatively tailored black blazer into a chic dinner jacket by pinning a delicate rhinestone-and-pearl brooch to its lapel. Conversely, the same black blazer becomes vibrant and casual when you add a colourful silk scarf at your neck.

Accessory Chic means knowing what clothes look best on you and work best for you—given your figure, colouring, and lifestyle—as well as knowing how to put the best looks together on a limited budget. To do this fast, and with savoir faire, you first need to assemble a basic wardrobe that has the maximum amount of versatility.

Integrate your basic wardrobe by selecting classic, versatile garments; you'll be able to coordinate outfits appropriate for both work and social situations.

Rethinking Your Wardrobe

First, make a good, long study of the clothes in your closet. Separate garments that are prints or patterns from those that are solids. If you're like most people, you'll probably have a fairly mismatched assortment.

Now, evaluate your clothes to see how many of them actually work together as outfits. Run a check on your blouses; do they complement your blazers, jumpers, pants, and skirts? Look for any imbalances in your wardrobe; for instance, you own ten jumpers, but only two of them are appropriate for work. Do you have a few pairs of classic, well-made shoes and boots? Can a couple of them do double duty for office and evening wear? As for leisure garments, do you have enough outfits to get you through all seasons and occasions? Asking questions like these will help you isolate what works in your wardrobe. You'll also discover its weak spots.

Depending on your lifestyle, it may help to separate your wardrobe into several distinct categories: autumn and winter work clothes; autumn and winter leisurewear; spring and summer work clothes; spring and summer leisurewear. You may also need to budget in sportswear and evening wear as categories. This exercise will probably uncover even more imbalances in your clothes collection.

To help you correct weak spots and imbalances, here is a basic wardrobe guide for every possible category.

AUTUMN AND WINTER WORK WARDROBE

▶ ONE CLASSICALLY tailored wool or wool blend suit with skirt. This should be in a dark colour that complements your skin tone; choose between blue, gray, brown, and black for the most versatility. The suit must be tastefully designed and well-cut for your figure type. Avoid anything that is overdetailed with bows, chains, unnecessary trim, or faddish collars or buttons.

▶ ONE SIMPLY tailored wool or wool blend pantsuit. Very often, you can find jackets that come with both a matching skirt and pants. If it fits well, you should seriously consider purchasing it—for its versatility and simplicity.

▶ ONE OR two pairs of gray, black, camel, or blue wool flannel pants that are complementary to the jacket of the pantsuit. As with the pantsuit, these pants should be straight-legged and uncuffed.

▶ EIGHT BLOUSES. A few Oxford cloth button-downs in pink, white, blue, and subtle stripes are good to start with. These will carry over into your spring work wardrobe. Add some classically designed cotton or lightweight wool blouses in solid seasonal colours; naturally, they should be chosen to coordinate with all your other suits and pants. You also need at least one solid-coloured silk blouse, preferably in ivory, gray, black, or navy. If your budget allows, a subtly patterned silk blouse will coordinate well with your suit and pants.

▶ TWO EXTRA skirts in wool, or a wool/polyester blend. Both should be in solid colours that coordinate with your suit jacket or extra blazer.

▶ THREE JUMPERS. Whether they are one hundred percent wool, angora, cashmere, cotton, or blends, they must be warm, solid-coloured, and appropriate with your suits.

▶ ONE CLASSICALLY cut wool blazer in blue, gray, brown, or black. A tweed blazer is a fashion perennial and a durable investment.

▶ ONE DURABLE, simply designed winter coat in camel, blue, or black. Black is a good choice if you find a coat that can also be worn for dressy occasions. Another sensible option is a navy blue, duster-style coat, which looks especially well with business clothes. Whichever you choose, the coat should be street-length—long enough to cover your dresses and skirts.

▶ ONE RAINCOAT that can also serve as a topcoat in spring and fall. Cotton poplin and twill are the sturdiest fabric choices. The classic, khaki, double-breasted, and belted trench coat looks great on everybody. If you buy one, be sure that it comes with a well-constructed, detachable lining. (A detachable lining is the secret to an all-weather coat.) You may also consider reversible coats—wool on one side and cotton twill or raincoat fabric on the other.

This jacket's timeless tailoring invites a variety of accessory styles. Always choose clothes that you can dress up or down as the occasion demands and the mood suits you.

Purchase clothes in natural fibers to get extra mileage out of your wardrobe. You'll be more comfortably dressed for tricky, in-between season temperatures.

AUTUMN AND WINTER LEISURE WEAR

▶ TWO PAIRS of jeans or work pants.

▶ ONE PAIR of casual, heavy cotton pants in a neutral, basic colour such as khaki.

▶ ONE INFORMAL skirt in a solid, seasonal colour.

▶ ONE PAIR of running shoes or sneakers.

▶ ONE PAIR of loafers or low-heeled casual shoes.

▶ ONE WOOL turtleneck jumper in a solid colour.

▶ AT LEAST two medium-weight to heavy-weight sweaters. You may want to buy one as an outer wrap—roomy enough to fit over a blouse and a medium-weight sweater. Again, solid-coloured sweaters make for a more varied wardrobe.

▶ AT LEAST three tailored blouses for week-end and after-work dressing.

SPRING AND SUMMER WORK WARDROBE

▶ ONE COTTON, linen, or seersucker suit. Synthetic fibers do not breathe and, therefore, are uncomfortable in warmer weather, so avoid them at all costs. Keep this in mind for the rest of your spring and summer wardrobe, too.

▶ TWO NATURAL-fiber dresses. Possible styles are: shirtwaists, T-shirt dresses, sleeveless sundresses, or long sheaths slit at the sides.

▶ TWO COTTON, linen, or natural-fiber-blend skirts.

▶ ONE DENIM skirt. Blue denim is now an accepted, classic fabric for a working wardrobe. Depending on your office environment, you may want to purchase a denim skirt in an above-the-knee—or even a mini—length. If the people in your industry and office dress casually, then obviously

The right combination of textured accessories will tastefully enhance any "conservative" outfit.

you have more leeway in choosing skirts and dresses.

▶ AS MANY T-shirts, cotton blouses, and lightweight jumpers as you can afford, in a palette of colours that complements your suit, skirts, and pants.

▶ THREE PAIRS of lightweight pants, in linen, cotton, and natural fiber blends only. Pants that come to slightly above the ankle with slits at the sides are very comfortable.

▶ ONE LIGHTWEIGHT, well-cut blazer that harmonizes with your skirts, dresses, and pants.

▶ ONE LIGHTWEIGHT, solid-coloured cardigan sweater that will keep you warm in an air-conditioned office or restaurant.

Spring and Summer Leisure Wear

▶ SEVERAL PAIRS of comfortable, wide-legged cotton or linen shorts in summery colours.

▶ A SLEEVELESS cotton jumpsuit that is roomy enough to fit a T-shirt underneath in cooler weather. Have one in a stretchy sweatshirt-type material for a more versatile garment.

▶ TWO OR three cotton tank tops for beach wear and hot days in town.

▶ A LIGHTWEIGHT beach cover-up, such as a gauzy tunic or cotton "big shirt." Try to find one you also can wear with shorts and jeans.

▶ LIGHTWEIGHT COTTON knit pants for evening dressing. Wear these with a tank top and a cotton sweater for stylish between-season comfort.

Year-Round Sportswear

Obviously, the type of sportswear you require is contingent on how active a life-style you lead, and, of course, how much money you can spend on this kind of clothing. When shopping for sportswear, remember that natural-fiber, loose-fitting clothes are an absolute must for comfort and safety. Physical exertion of any kind causes perspiration and friction between clothing and skin, so don't negate the benefits of working out by causing unnecessary skin irritations or infections.

The Basics

Here are a few guidelines for assembling a basic sportswear wardrobe:

▶ A ONE HUNDRED percent cotton sweatsuit in a loose-fitting size can take you through tennis, jogging, aerobics classes, and gymwork year-round. A sweatsuit is also the most comfortable outfit to wear when cleaning house.

▶ A HOODED, 100 percent cotton sweatshirt for winter wear and/or beachwear.

▶ AN ASSORTMENT of short- and long-sleeved T-shirts to wear under your sweatsuit.

▶ AT LEAST one cotton leotard. Although synthetic leotards are still popular, they do not allow perspiration to evaporate.

▶ AT LEAST one pair of loosely cut cotton or nylon running shorts.

▶ ONE PAIR of sports shoes, appropriate for the type of workout you do.

This basic black dress has an '80s attitude—tailored and sexy in one smoothly constructed line. Look for a black dress that will remain stylish over the years.

Evening Wear

Since the late 1920s, every fashionable woman has owned at least one "basic black dress." This wonderfully versatile garment evolved out of the average woman's need for an all-purpose, tasteful dress that would be perfectly appropriate for all daytime situations. Then it was discovered that when properly accessorized with real or costume jewellery, the basic black dress could become suitably elegant for cocktail parties and other semiformal evening occasions. You should have one in wool, silk, or linen; a wool jersey, in fact, would probably be the most durable choice. Modern variations on the basic black dress include leather or velvet skirts teamed with coordinated black blazers or jackets, or black cashmere or angora sweater dresses. Ensembles like these can be dazzlingly chic if you wear them with the right belts, jewellery, scarves, and hosiery. It all depends on how dramatic a style you're after. For optimum wearability, though, remember to choose a dress that has simple, easy lines, one that will be unobtrusive enough for the office yet easily dressed up for after-work engagements.

If a black suit is part of your winter work wardrobe, chances are it can function as flawless evening wear as well. There are countless ways to accessorize such an outfit. And, if your budget allows, another timeless, unadorned dress in black, navy, dark brown, or gray would be a valuable asset to your total look. A pink, red, or purple dress also might be worth buying for the lift it will bring to your wardrobe and your spirits.

Now that you've assembled the basics, you're ready to start accessorizing from the top down, while developing your personal style. Fashion can be bought, but one must possess style. The good news is that proper accessories put you in charge of your style, and enable you to look your best in every situation.

From eyewear to jewellery to undergarments; footwear, millinery, and umbrellas, ACCESSORY CHIC offers detailed examples of how to outfit yourself creatively with quality fashion extras. Moreover, if you're on a budget, you'll learn how to choose accessories that mark you as dressed for success.

Study your wardrobe for evening, then dramatize it with imaginative accessories. Look at fashion magazines and clothing catalogues for ideas on how to add nighttime dash. Try mixing jewellery styles as in the necklace, earring, hat pin, and bracelet combination to the right. The styles on the far right illustrate how boldly proportioned jewellery will glamourize simply designed daytime separates into nighttime looks.

Focus on Eyewear

Chapter One:

Although many women readily spend money on accessories such as jewellery, shoes, hosiery, and hats, when it comes to buying eyeglasses, they settle for the least expensive frames they can find. This attitude is decidedly unwise. Glasses are more than an accessory: They are a necessity. Because they protect your precious eyesight, your glasses are vitally important to your health. They also contribute to what the famed fashion designer Coco Chanel called "the total look."

There was a time when there were but a few eyeglass frames to choose from. Not surprisingly, women who needed to wear eyeglasses considered them an unfortunate and unfashionable necessity. Modern times have wrought a shift in this attitude, however, and today eyeglasses are not only fashionable—they are even considered high fashion.

Now you have thousands of frame shapes and colours to choose from. For example, there are myriad variations of squares, ovals, and rounds. You can even choose from styles that mix different shapes, such as those with round tops and octagonal bottoms. Additionally, frames come in multitoned colour combinations and patterns. Famous beauties like Sophia Loren, Gloria Vanderbilt, and Diane von Furstenberg all wear glasses themselves and design distinctive collections of "eyewear" for today's woman.

Different Eyeglass Lenses

No discussion of eyewear would be complete without a quick rundown of the varieties of eyeglass lenses that are on the market. To begin with, all lenses are made from impact-resistant plastic or glass. As plastic is considerably lighter, it is a much more popular material than glass. The one drawback to plastic lenses is that they scratch more easily than glass ones. Although some ophthalmologists believe that glass lenses filter out more of the sun's ultraviolet rays, they will not necessarily spare you eyestrain when you're outdoors. For intense sunlight and glare, the best type of lens is a polarized one, preferably mirrored. Polarized lenses reduce bright light, so they are invaluable for the beach, skiing, or—if you're so inclined—the desert.

For all-purpose indoor/outdoor eyewear, phototropic lenses are the most sensible and economical choice. These are light-sensitive lenses that change from an almost clear tint to a dark one depending on the light conditions. Buying one pair of phototropic lenses would save you the trouble and expense of buying a pair of sunglasses. Gradient density lenses are darker on the top and lighter on the bottom; excellent for driving and sailing, they're also a good choice for joggers.

LENS TINTS

Tinted lenses are available in several forms and are graded on a scale of one to five, solid to gradient. Five is the darkest, and as such, it's the tint most often used in sunglasses. Solid tints have the same degree of colour throughout the lens. Multicoloured tints can combine two or three colours in one lens.

Remember, the asset of tinted lenses is that they emphasize your eyes in the same way eye makeup can, but be careful with the colour and gradation you choose. For example, a solid rose tone will make your eyes look pink and sickly. Never pick light gray or green tints, for they usually emphasize pale or tired skin and lines under the eyes. If you decide on a rose or mauvish tint, the colour must be graded from dark rose down to light. Another key cosmetic advantage of tinted lenses to keep in mind: Tinting will hide and minimize the look of thick or unusually strong prescription lenses.

As for nighttime tints, opticians recommend a multicoloured tint: blue tints in the center of the lens to emphasize the whites of the eyes, with a rosy or peach tone on the bottom to soften any lines or shadows underneath the eyes. The top part of the lens could be either light gray or light mauve.

Frame Selection Guidelines

With such a diverse selection on the market, determining which eyeglasses are best for you involves more than choosing a frame that complements the shape of your face. Besides bone structure, other important factors to consider are the size of your eyes—large or small—and whether they are wide- or close-set. Your hairstyle, hair colour, and skin tone also should affect your decision, as should your recreational activities and work environment. Some women opt to have two or more different pairs of glasses—for work and for leisure—but you can easily find one all-purpose frame.

When selecting eyeglasses, try to stand in front of a full-length mirror, for the frame must be proportionate to both your face *and* your height and weight. This is also the only way to get a definite idea of what frames suit you best. Remember to look for glasses that play up your facial features; very often, women with well-proportioned faces select glasses that are less than flattering to their particular eye type, thereby giving their faces a misproportioned look. For instance, if you have small, close-set eyes, a large frame that reaches the sides of your face will only accentuate the fact that your eyes are close to your nose; a smaller frame would be more flattering. Conversely, if you have large, wide-set eyes, a frame that's too small or narrow will make your eyes seem even farther apart from each other and from your nose.

EYEWEAR STYLES

As with all fashionable apparel, there are a few perennially popular styles of eyeglasses—classic frames that suit almost every situation, season, and wardrobe. Before considering any style, however, ask yourself some key questions about your lifestyle and wardrobe.

▶ IS YOUR professional environment casual or conservative? Your glasses should not clash with your office climate. If you work in a fast-paced, stylish office, obviously you have more latitude when it comes to choosing which sunglasses and glasses to wear.

▶ ARE YOU an eclectic dresser who mixes vintage clothes and/or accessories with contemporary clothing? If so, your glasses should be chosen with special care; you want their scale and proportion to be in sync with your clothes, shoes, hats, and jewellery.

▶ WHAT KIND of image do you want to convey to others? Do you have a good idea of what your "total look" is? You need to develop self-knowledge like this in order to attain the look that's perfect for you.

Horn-rimmed glasses have been in and out of style for over a century. Literary women such as Virginia Woolf wore them, although the style primarily was worn by men. In the late 1970s, however, the movie actress Diane Keaton gave pop-culture credibility to horn-rims by wearing them in her Academy Award winning performance in *Annie Hall*. These rounded frames became a funky but chic eyeglass style for women, and soon horn-rims were available in a palette of colours ranging from traditional salmon pink and tortoiseshell tones to blues, greens, and violets. Simultaneously stylish and serious, horn-rims suit many face shapes and are befitting to most women's lifestyles and wardrobes. No matter the size of the frames,

Intriguingly styled or diamond-encrusted frames will at times be a reflection of your image and mood.

however, they must be coordinated carefully with accessories of appropriate size that mix harmoniously and pull your look together. If you find that this classic frame shape is too conservative or mannish for you, there are several updated variations on horn-rims now available that may suit you better; perhaps a thinner, more delicate frame with more angular lenses is the answer.

Another perennially popular frame style is the wire-rimmed aviator, which started out as a sunglass frame and then became popular for corrective glasses. Aviators come in a multitude of materials and colours besides the traditional gold and silver wire rims. A well-stocked optician will carry everything from black metal to brightly coloured, plastic-coated wire rims. Like many classic eyeglass frames on the market today, aviators also come in a type of plastic that is textured and coloured so that it resembles wood. One particularly attractive style is a wire-rimmed frame with rimless bottoms. The lack of metal around the bottom half of the lens makes your glasses less obtrusive and, therefore, easier to accessorize. If you wear a variety of metallic or colourful earrings, this may be the style for you.

A classic, delicate frame such as narrow tortoiseshell flatters most face shapes. Any

If you wear earrings and/or necklaces frequently, bring some with you when you are choosing your frame. You'll be sure to select a frame that suits your total look.

large lens in a light frame complements small and large facial structures alike. If you're after a more modern shape, curved oblongs, horn-rims, narrow oval wraparounds, oversized squares with rounded corners are some of the choices. When selecting from this myriad of frame shapes, try to imagine how they'll look with your office clothes, dressy outfits, and casual wear. Your glasses should be attractive and stylish, but versatility is your first priority.

SIZING UP FRAMES

Here are some hints on the frames that are most flattering to particular face shapes:

▶ ROUND FACE: The number one rule for you is to avoid roundish frames, for they will only emphasize the fullness of your face. Instead, look for a frame that will give you a more angular appearance. The lens area should not be too wide, as this will also exaggerate your face shape.

▶ PEAR FACE: This face shape is thick at the bottom—across the jaw and chin area—and narrow across the eyes. Accordingly, you should try to find glasses with broad rims that give a wider look to the top portion of your face. Avoid rimless or thin wire frames, as these will emphasize the wrong part of your face.

▶ HEART FACE: This kind of face has a wide forehead and eye area; the jaw and chin are much narrower. A good choice for you is a frame that is heavier or rounder at the bottom, giving your features a more balanced look.

▶ OVAL FACE: The Mona Lisa exemplifies this face shape. The oval face is ideally balanced, with the top half equal to the bottom. Consequently, you will probably find a variety of frames that suit you. Should your face be on the heavy side, chose a thin frame that is slightly angular to even out your features. If your face is thin, go for a frame that gives an illusion of fullness; one that is slightly rounded would perhaps suit you better than a geometric style.

▶ SQUARE FACE: This face has a well-defined, angular bone structure. The jaw is strong; the forehead and brow bones are also squared-off. Try to find a curvy or rounded frame to soften the angularity of your features. The outer corners of the frame should span your cheekbone, which will minimize a strong jaw and give your face a gentler more rounded look.

Plastic tortoiseshell frames complement professional wardrobes as well as alluring evening outfits.

It is advisable to consult an optometrist, optician, or ophthalmologist whenever you're investing in new frames. Never buy frames for prescription glasses in boutiques or department stores; when you bring them to the

Frames that are keyed to hair colour and skin tone will give you a fashionable pulled-together look.

optician, you may find that the lenses you need cannot be made to fit the shape of the frame you chose. Some prescriptions become distorted in a large size lens, while small lenses usually cannot accommodate a strong prescription.

CHECKLIST FOR CHOOSING A FRAME COLOUR TO MATCH YOUR HAIR COLOUR AND SKIN TONE

To save time and worry while you're matching your eyeglass frames to your natural colouring, here are some practical suggestions for coordinating the two:

▶ BRUNETTE HAIR and fair skin: Gold, copper, salmon, light blue, turquoise, and tortoiseshell are good colours to start with. Avoid dark, harsh colours, since these will accentuate your colouring to the extreme.

▶ BRUNETTE HAIR and dark skin: Silver, gold, pink, translucent, and amber frames will brighten up your colouring. Browns, blues, and blacks will probably work against you.

▶ RED HAIR and rosy complexion: Silver, gold, tortoiseshell, medium blue, and burgundy red are most suitable for your unusual colouring. Steer clear of anything in the beige to brown range. Mauve and purple are also not for you.

▶ BLONDE HAIR and fair skin: Gold, copper, and bronze metal can be quite complementary. Also, try dark browns, black, blue, and lilac. You want to avoid translucent frames and anything else that's pastel or crystalline in tone. Tortoiseshell always seems to go with blond hair and fair colouring—give it a try.

▶ GRAY HAIR and any skin tone: Silver, brown, black, medium to dark blue, salmon, and bright red are your best bets. Forget about translucent frames or those in pale colours. They'll make your skin look pale and washed out. Go for something contrasting and colourful instead.

Caring for Eyeglasses

As your glasses are an essential tool for living as well as a significant financial investment, it makes sense to care for them responsibly. Wash your glasses at least once a day with soap and water. Wipe them dry with a tissue or linen towel reserved for this purpose. If you have oily skin and your glasses feel a bit greasy by the end of the day, spray them with an ammonia-based cleaner and rinse them before washing them off with soap and water. For quick, in-between cleanups, lens tissues are a handy solution. They are available in small packets you can carry in your purse at most chemists and photo-supply stores; carrying a packet of them will insure clear vision at all times.

Another way to protect your glasses is by carrying them in a durable plastic case that is hard enough to resist minor shocks such as being dropped on the floor. Remember that plastic lenses scratch easily, so never place your glasses on a surface with the lenses facing down. Finally, have your glasses adjusted every three months by an optician. Whether the temples need tightening or the lenses are a bit loose, taking care of minor maintenance matters will make your glasses last longer and insures maximum comfort.

Mirrored lenses are a stylish shield against harsh sun rays. A veneer of slick mystery, their reflective surface hides your eyes from the world—no gaze can penetrate the masklike mirrors.

Sunglasses or Cool Shades

Besides protecting your eyes from sun, sea, wind, and sand, sunglasses can automatically change your appearance like no other accessory. Depending on the type of frames and lenses you wear, sunglasses instantly can make you look mysterious, sporty, demure, or drop-dead chic.

Since sunglasses are a necessity and not a luxury item, your main concern should be the colour and quality of the lens. Keep these guidelines in mind when buying your sunglasses. Any sunglasses should screen out seventy percent of the natural light. The glasses you wear at the beach or in the snow where the sun is more intense should block out eighty-five percent to ninety percent of the sun's rays. Sunglasses will help prevent eyestrain, premature wrinkles, and crow's feet as well.

Jazzy sunglasses give any outfit a de luxe finish.

"I have six pairs of sunglasses that I've collected over the years," says Jeanette Lee, who works in a New York publishing house. "Two of them were originally my father's glasses; I had the lenses removed so the optician could replace them with my prescription. The other pairs I have came from different thrift shops and vintage-clothing boutiques."

Jeanette's assortment of sunglasses allows her to put together—ingeniously and inexpensively—various unique looks. Her 1950s-style black wraparounds, for instance, are worn mainly on the weekends with casual clothes. Yet they also put a slick finishing touch on certain work outfits, like a black linen suit that she wears in spring and summer. Jeanette suggests that you ask any family members if they have cast-off glasses that might fit you before you sink any money into a new pair of sunglasses. For instance, your grandmother's pearl-encrusted, cat's-eye sunglasses could now be resurrected as offbeat, elegant shades for your more stylish outfits. Otherwise, keep an eye out, at rummage sales and flea markets, for distinctive vintage specs you can convert.

As you can see, it's a good idea to save any and all pairs of eyeglasses for future recycling. In fact, there's a process for converting glasses into sunglasses that is fast and inexpensive. It's called "dipping," and it can help you get extra use out of prescription glasses that you've been wearing for some time. The lenses are tinted whatever shade you desire and will stay that colour indefinitely. The prescription is not affected by this process.

COORDINATING YOUR SUNGLASSES WITH DIFFERENT LOOKS

For simplicity's sake, coordinate your sunglasses with your basic work, leisure, and sports wardrobes. To avoid a cluttered, over-accessorized look, only wear jewellery of proportion and colour that works discreetly with your sunglasses. Sometimes less is more, and this is especially true if you wear glasses with other accessories. But exactly how do you determine which sunglasses to wear with a specific outfit? Keep in mind the essential character and distinctiveness of each pair. For instance, think twice before you team mirrored, high-tech sunglasses with a conventional work or leisure wardrobe. The wrong sunglasses could create a disjointed, uneasy appearance and make a less than positive impression on others. The line, colour, and spirit of your sunglasses must be consistent with your total look.

The casual flair of these sunglasses is the final touch to a sporty outfit.

Contact lenses come in various styles, colours, and forms. Visit an optometrist to find out which type best serves your fashion and optical needs.

Contact Lenses

Impressive innovations in contact-lens design and comfort have occurred in the last decade. Some of the more recent breakthroughs are: bifocal lenses; extended-wear lenses that stay in the eyes for up to a month or more; soft lenses that can intensify or change the colour of your eyes. The original hard lens is still popular, as it's quite easy to care for and sterilize; so is the combination hard/soft lens. Prices for soft contact lenses are now equal to—sometimes less than—what you would pay for a brand new pair of glasses. Always do comparison shopping before purchasing a pair of contact lenses. The market is very competitive now; you can find a bargain if you do a little investigative research beforehand.

Many women lead life-styles that make glasses impractical. Contact lenses may be an excellent option for you if you play a lot of sports or spend several hours a day reading. Contact-lens wearers enjoy sharper peripheral vision, and if your eyesight is especially weak, contacts might be a better choice for you than glasses. Although contact-lens hygiene procedures, when followed properly, remove all bacteria and effectively sterilize the lenses, some wearers still experience minor irritations or become prone to eye infections like conjunctivitis. Because a contact lens is a foreign body in the eye that deprives your cornea of oxygen, you must be careful not to wear them for too long (unless you have special extended-wear models) or in situations where you can harm your eyes, such as in a chlorine swimming pool or at the beach on a windy day. One important note to contact-lens wearers: Never use commercial eye drops to brighten your eyes while wearing contact lenses. These commercial solutions are filled with chemicals that can damage your contacts and your eyes.

Most opticians carry a full line of hard- and soft-lensed contacts that are tinted in blue, green, brown, violet, and hazel. For the most natural look, select a tint that will harmonize with your skin tone and hair colour. Then again, you may want to cultivate a dramatic, violet-eyed gaze instead of staying true to your naturally brown eyes. This is a subjective matter, so use your better judgment. Tinted lenses occasionally can be unflattering. Sometimes they make your eyes overpower your other features, resulting in a doll-faced look.

Other Eye Apparel and Accessories

Another eyewear style you could adopt are lorgnettes—long popular with glamourous women who enjoy adding a little flourish to their impaired eyesight! Lorgnettes are halfway between practical eyewear and exquisite jewellery. Ivory or silver pearlized lorgnettes look wonderful on most women and accessorize easily with earrings, necklaces, and bracelets. Because lorgnettes add a dash of eccentricity to your appearance, they might not be right for every situation. For evening wear, however, they look extremely smart.

If you are less than fond of wearing glasses all the time but have no alternative, you could try wearing a decorative chain on your eyeglasses. This way, your spectacles can hang in style when you don't want to wear them. Eyeglass chains come in gold, silver, and other metals; they're also available in natural-fiber cords, stretchable coloured elastics, and various types of plastic designs. You can easily afford to buy different pairs for different occasions: daytime, parties, the opera, and other formal occasions. Variety stores usually have a large selection of chains that cost less than those sold by opticians. Other places to find eyeglass chains are flea markets, department stores, and vintage clothing shops.

Mirrored sports glasses are vital for snow, sea, and desert conditions, as well as being fabulous accessories for casual and evening expeditions.

LEGWEAR AND LINGERIE

Chapter Two:

Although the French word "lingerie" originally meant linen garments, we know it today as a synonym for women's underdressings. Whether a bra, a half-slip, a camisole, or support pantyhose, the lingerie you wear greatly determines the way your clothing hangs on your body—the way your body looks inside your clothes. After all, lingerie and legwear are vital, though often neglected, elements of your total look, and they contribute significantly, though not obviously to the overall impression you make on others.

To enhance your figure as much as possible, all legwear and lingerie must fit smoothly and invisibly under your garments. For instance, nothing looks worse than a fluid silk blouse worn with a thick-seamed bra underneath. The sheer elegance of silk should never be marred by unbecoming outlines. Likewise, a slit skirt which reveals an inappropriately cut slip instead of a flash of leg is equally unattractive. If your pantyhose are too heavy for the skirt or dress you are wearing, the material will hang wrong, spoiling the line of the outfit.

The great thing about legwear and lingerie is that they enhance your wardrobe in both visible and invisible ways, without costing too much. As the empress of twentieth-century fashion, Diana Vreeland, once wrote, "...people have too many clothes...Change your stockings—wear other-coloured stockings and change your whole look!" Mrs. Vreeland edited Vogue magazine for two decades, so she obviously knows a thing or two about dressing smart and accessorizing with flair. If you've honed your basic wardrobe down to the essentials, then you're in the perfect position to start enhancing your clothes with all manner of legwear and lingerie, beginning with pantyhose.

When shopping for lingerie, play it safe and wear the sort of clothes that will be worn over the bra, slip, or all-in-one that you're going to buy. For this reason, think twice before ordering undergarments through mail-order catalogues. Sure, it's convenient, but you may wind up with lingerie that is impractical for your wardrobe. Although it's impossible to try on pantyhose or socks before you buy them, be sure to open the package or ask to see the display or sample pair to check the colour, weight, and texture.

Pantyhose

Any pantyhose you wear should be selected with the key elements of colour, texture, pattern, and thickness in mind. Again, try to shop for stockings when you're wearing the dress or separates that you need to match.

PANTYHOSE BASICS

Here are descriptions of the wide variety of pantyhose available:

▶ NEUTRAL OR nude pantyhose ostensibly all come in neutral tones, but some are darker than others and finding a hue that matches your skin tone can be tricky. Avoid hose that are so dark they make your legs look artificially tan. Stick to the lighter shades, and you'll look fine.

▶ SHEER PANTYHOSE slim the legs and are particularly alluring for nighttime wear. If you want to pull out all the stops, black sheer hose with metallic or rhinestoned seams are an ultra-dressy accessory for your basic black dress or skirt-and-jacket ensemble. Blue, gray, beige, and white sheers are excellent hose for many daytime outfits, as well.

▶ OPAQUE PANTYHOSE are usually more durable than sheers, for they are a thicker weight of nylon. There are also one hundred percent cotton opaque pantyhose on the market now. Unless your opaques are in dark tones such as brown, purple, navy, or black, their colours will make your legs appear thicker.

▶ PATTERNED PANTYHOSE come in everything from zebra stripes to tiny, modern geometric prints. When coordinating patterned pantyhose with an outfit, your main concern should be to find a pattern that blends well with the colour and texture of your clothing and shoes. If it doesn't, your look will be all wrong. As with all accessories, think about your physical proportions before buying patterned hose. While flattering for women who have long or too-skinny legs, patterned tights might be a mistake if your legs are on the heavy or short side.

▶ TEXTURED PANTYHOSE come in myriad styles, the tried-and-true classic being the fishnet. Long worn by dancers onstage and off, fishnets are an inexpensive way to give your evening outfit a *de luxe* finish. Since they are highly provocative and illusory, they're not exactly appropriate for daytime wear! Other popular textures are horizontal or vertical ribs, puckered designs in various shapes, *point d'ésprit* (woven dots and flourishes), fans and diamonds, and, of course, lace. The perennial stocking of choice for little girls to wear with their party dresses, lace hose are now enjoying a significant revival as fashionable legwear for women. Why? Because lace, when compared to other textured hose, is the most decorative, dramatic, and interesting.

▶ SUPPORT HOSE are a lifesaver to you if your legs ache by the end of the day, and they also combat varicose veins. Support hose come in a variety of colours and textures and are available in department stores, and lingerie shops.

▶ EXTRA-WIDE PANTYHOSE for full-figured women come in a wide variety of styles. Look for these in department stores or maternity and lingerie shops.

Delicate dots, glittery rhinestone, frothy lace: pantyhose come in dozens of exuberantly ornamental designs. Patterned pantyhose with a black, white, or metallic background are a chic asset to evening dressing.

Pantyhose Checklist

Resist the temptation to buy any and all pantyhose that strike your fancy; chances are you don't need them. Keep your wardrobe organized and coordinated at all times so you save yourself from unnecessary expenses. All you really need are about a dozen pairs of pantyhose:

▶ TWO PAIRS nude hose.

▶ TWO PAIRS daytime sheers.

▶ TWO PAIRS nighttime sheers.

▶ TWO PAIRS coloured opaques.

▶ TWO PAIRS autumn/winter patterns (dark).

▶ TWO PAIRS spring/summer patterns (pastel or light-coloured).

▶ ONE PAIR each black and white lace.

How and Where to Buy Pantyhose for Less

Most department stores have seasonal hosiery sales where you can buy several pairs of pantyhose at a marked discount. Watch for sales in early fall, late winter, and early spring. Another way you can save on pantyhose is to purchase them at variety and discount stores, instead of at specialty shops or department stores.

Petite or thin women can definitely save on hosiery if they buy their stockings in the young girls' department instead of the women's. Many of the styles for girls are just as suitable for young or even middle-aged women, so if you're small of stature, by all means, take home a pair and see if they fit. If you are trying to cultivate a unique style, an added advantage of wearing girls' pantyhose is that very few other women will have stockings that look like yours!

Other prime places to look for pantyhose are hosiery and dancewear shops and outlets. You'll find a variety of colours, patterns, and textures there that is staggering, and the prices at these stores (even when they're not having a sale) are usually quite reasonable, even better in quantities of a dozen or more.

Use textured pantyhose as a striking counterpoint to your other accessories and garments. Lacy pantyhose paired with patent leather shoes decorate your legs with sleek chic.

Stockings and garter belts finished with high heels are the ultimate in festive dressing.

Caring For Your Pantyhose

▶ IF YOU snag your pantyhose and they start to run, don't throw them away. You can make them wearable again by brushing a little clear nail polish onto the end of the run and letting it dry. Make sure the end of the run is completely covered. You can now wear them under pants or long skirts that conceal the damaged area.

▶ ALWAYS WASH pantyhose in a delicate soap and water solution after wearing. Rinse them well and let them hang dry; wringing the water from them will stretch the material.

▶ WOMEN WHO wear pointed shoes often find the toes of their pantyhose in tatters after a long day of work or a night on the town. Whenever this happens, recycle your pantyhose by cutting them off at the ankle. Wear hose without feet under skirts or pants with colourful or contrasting socks. Layered hosiery is the latest style and adds dimension to any outfit. It is also extremely flattering on thin-legged or small-boned women.

Stockings and Garter Belts

Silk stockings worn with a lace and satin garter belt are the height of sensuous, glamourous dressing. Admittedly, old-fashioned stockings and garter belts can be fairly expensive accessories. But if you can afford them, they are much more comfortable than nylon pantyhose. They allow you greater freedom of movement, and because they don't cover your bottom half, they are much cooler than regular pantyhose. You'll find the best selection of stockings and belts at major department stores or lingerie shops. Legwear and lingerie like this always give an invisible lift to your festive attire and attitude. Stockings and a garter belt can pull your look together with stylish elegance.

34 • Accessory Chic

The first priority of exercise tights and leggings is that they are comfortable and provide freedom of movement. If you exercise strenuously, cotton tights and cotton or wool leggings will absorb perspiration better than synthetic materials.

Tights

While pantyhose are lightweight and most suitable for work and formal wardrobe, tights are durable and appropriate for casual wear and exercise workouts. Here are some specific suggestions:

▶ DANCE TIGHTS come in nylon, acrylic, cotton, or a blend of these. They're available in hundreds of patterns and colours.

▶ TIGHTS WITHOUT feet (they stop at the ankle) can also do double duty between your exercise and casual wardrobes. Many of the footless designs are perfectly appropriate worn casually under skirts. Wear them with delicate ankle socks and flat shoes, and you've got a stylish, unusual look.

▶ TIGHTS WITH stirrups are another style of exercise tights that can add dash to your outfits by highlighting a well-turned ankle or an attractive pair of shoes. Stirrups worn with casual flat shoes make a short skirt look sporty. Or, wear them with sleekly cut shoes under a body-hugging knit dress or tunic when you go out dancing.

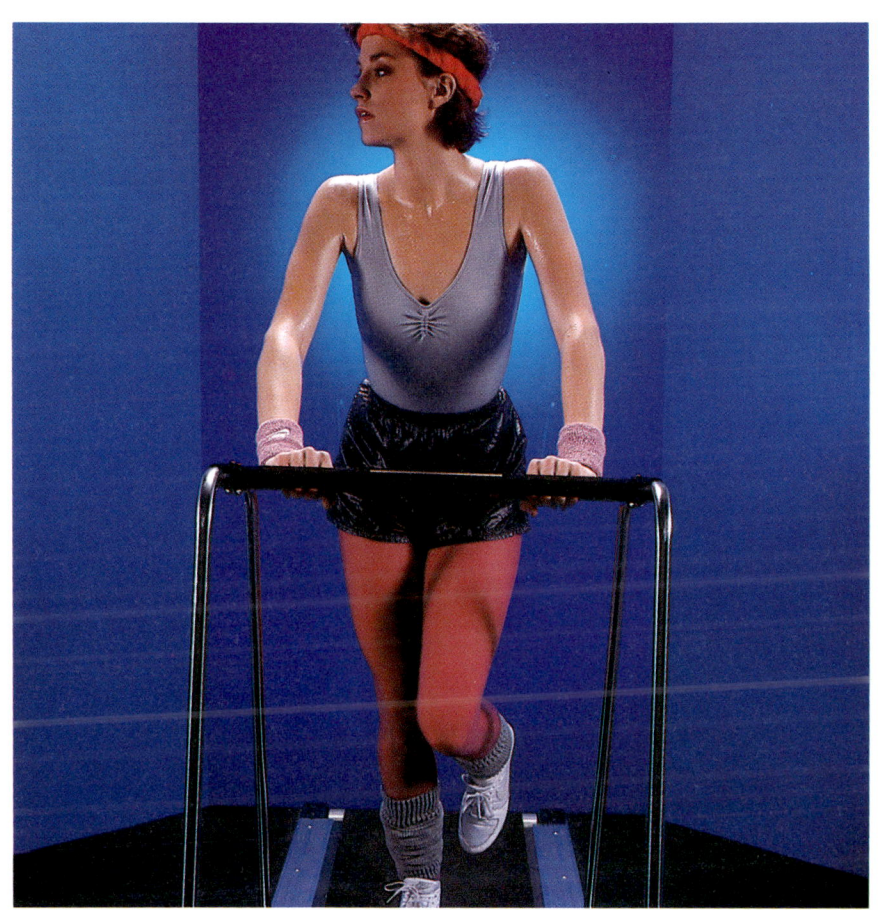

Light and Heavy Leggings

"Leggings" come in all fabrics, weaves, and colours. They usually stop at the ankle and can be light enough for summer wear. In fact, many women wear colourfully dyed army surplus long johns as warm-weather slacks, coordinated with any size T-shirt or tunic. They also look great under short skirts, if you fancy the layered look. Cotton long johns are also the best thing to wear under sweatpants for a cold winter's jog. They are absorbent and help retain body heat, keeping muscles warm and supple as you work out. Also, they make a thrifty choice as comfortable, warm pyjama bottoms.

If you wear skirts throughout winter, leggings over pantyhose will protect from chills, impaired blood circulation, even frostbite. Whether they come in two separate pieces like socks or are knitted together at the waist, wool leggings offer warmth and comfort without restricting ease of movement.

An excellent solution to other cold-weather wardrobe needs would be wool leg warmers or boot liners. If you know how to knit, you can stitch up a pair of leg warmers or full-length leggings that will last you forever. Remember that if you have great legs, you can show them to their best advantage in winter by wearing wool leggings with matching socks or knee-high hose. Add a pair of heeled shoes and a knit dress or an extra long sweater, and you've got a fashionable, warm, and distinctive outfit. Match your layered sweater look on top by tucking your pants into boot liners that peek from the top of your mid-calf-high boots.

Matching Pantyhose, Stockings, and Leggings with Different Looks

Worn with your pantsuits and skirts, sheer pantyhose give a slightly formal, dramatic finish to outfits. They're much sexier than opaque pantyhose. Additionally, you can use sheers to balance the heavy texture of a ribbed wool sweater, toning down the impact of your total look. You can also echo or offset the colours of your earrings, necklaces, or eyeglasses with sheer-colored hose.

If you love to make a colourful impression, opaque hose are one of your most effective accessories. Jazz up a plain gray or black suit with pink opaques; you'll still look dignified and professional, but with flair! For evening wear, team brightly hued opaques with dark separates or a basic black dress. Turquoise, cherry red, and violet make a black outfit go festive; white or silvery opaques are for more formal and subdued occasions. For springtime outfits, you can choose any pastel or primary colours. Remember that shocking colours like fluorescent pink or green are *very* bright, and faddish to boot. If you wear them, make sure that they don't overpower the rest of your clothes. (Fluorescents also come in sheer weaves, so maybe you should try them first.) Opaque pantyhose are an essential accessory for women who like to dress monochromatically.

Obviously, if you're adventurous enough to choose patterned pantyhose, you're after a visually arresting, artistic look. Don't spoil it all by wearing patterns that clash loudly with your clothes, jewellery, or shoes. By all means, experiment with mixing patterns. Pin-dot stockings can look great with a striped shirt and a solid-coloured skirt, for instance, but be careful to avoid combinations that are loud, busy, or confusing.

For colour and texture right down to your toes; to add a subtle, extra dimension to your separates; to emphasize beautiful leather or snakeskin shoes; this is what textured hose are for. Semi-sheer, vertical-ribbed hose classically complement skirts, suits, and unadorned dresses; they'll also make your legs look slimmer. Tightly crocheted weaves are the perfect match for knitted sweaters paired with wool or tweed skirts and suede shoes; they're also just right for softer fashions, such as cashmere and angora tops or dresses. Puckered, dotted, and other weaves can fill out slender legs. Pantyhose like these lend balance to heavy winter jumpers, giving a slim figure a unified proportion. Intricate, lacy designs add softness to sharply tailored dresses and separates. But stay away from white lace if your legs are on the muscular or heavy side. The colour and pattern will make them appear even larger. Black lace can be a fantastic contrast with a black velvet or leather skirt or for any romantic nighttime look. You could even key a whole outfit around your lace hose by wearing them with a flowing skirt, a lacy blouse, and pearl earrings.

Buy footless tights at dancewear shops and wear them with coloured socks or intriguingly textured anklets. Depending on the length of your skirt, complete the ensemble with high heels or flats. You can save extra money by purchasing several pairs of pantyhose at once in variety stores or hosiery outlets; take them home and cut off the feet yourself, then roll them to just slightly above your ankles.

Wear stirrup tights with a long sweater on top and matching pumps, flats, or high heels. You'll have a sporty, streamlined look that can be worn casual or dressed up with different accessories. Wool leggings can be worn the same way, with either a knitted dress or an extra long, body-hugging jumper. For warmth and comfort, wear pantyhose underneath the leggings.

Leg warmers, ankle leggings and boot liners all look nice with jeans, corduroys—even sweatpants. If you find leg warmers too constricting, ankle leggings stop at just under the knee and will give you the warmth you need. Boot liners peeking out of a pair of leather or suede boots add a touch of colour to your outfit; they also protect your pantyhose from snagging on the inside of your boots.

Wear cotton long johns as casual summer pants with sneakers and a T-shirt or an oversized, tailored shirt belted at the waist. Although many women wear long johns under full-cut skirts for extra warmth in the winter, they're not exactly the most attractive solution to cold-weather dressing. They are practical, so in the bitter cold wear them to work, but remove them when you arrive.

Legwear and Lingerie • 37

Ankle socks worn over pantyhose add kicky colour, dimension, and dazzle to mini- and longer skirt dressing. This is, however, a casual daytime style. For the mini-skirt outfit on the left, sexy sheer hose make a properly fetching fashion statement.

Knee-High Hose and Socks

Exuberant, nostalgic, zany, or classic—an eclectic array of knee-high hose and socks injects splendid energy into work, casual, and evening wardrobes.

When buying socks, it's always a good idea to picture in your mind the shoes, bags, and belts that you must coordinate them with. That much said, have fun sock shopping!

Knee-high hose are a must for a working woman's wardrobe. Perfect for wearing under pants in the warmer months, they're much more professional-looking than socks. Because many women find it uncomfortable and irritating to wear pantyhose under pants, knee-high hose are a welcome alternative. They're half the price of pantyhose, every inch as attractive, and definitely user-friendly. Don't forget that support hose also come in knee-high styles, as well. If you're on your feet all day, these will give you a needed lift. And when your knee-high hose are worn out, ball them up and stuff them into the toes of your shoes. This will help boots and shoes retain their shape while they lie in your closet.

Like most women, you probably wore drab, monotoned knee socks all through your youth. When you were old enough to stop wearing them, you did so without a second thought. Well, it's time to think again. Today's knee-sock styles are available in myriad colours, textures, and patterns. They're designed by fashion industry leaders like Norma Kamali, Mary Quant, and Christian Dior. You can even find knee socks in a rich array of fabrics; silk, cashmere, angora, and cotton/linen blends are just a few examples.

When shopping for socks, select them with an eye toward the specific. This means buying socks that will, of course, coordinate with separates and shoes; it also means picturing the clothes your socks must complement. For example, if you wear hats, scarves, gloves, or leg warmers that are in roughly the same area of the colour spectrum, you should have at least three pairs of socks that subtly accentuate these pieces.

Buy your warm and cold-weather socks with the same imaginative attitude you brought to selecting your other hosiery. You'll soon define a style of dressing that's completely your own. Inject individualistic colour and texture combinations into your wardrobe through your choice of socks. Mix socks, shoes, and separates despite—or because of—their contrasting qualities. Here are some ideas to get you going:

▶ TO LIVEN up a straight-cut linen or cotton seersucker skirt, add a pair of crochet-textured pastel anklets to flat shoes, such as loafers.

▶ TO GLAMOURIZE the look of a slinky summer dress, wear it with frilly lace anklets and high heels.

▶ TO PERSONALIZE a pair of classic walking shorts, wear colourfully patterned socks with sneakers or low-heeled T-strap shoes.

▶ TO ADD oomph to a drab sweatsuit, pick amusing patterns for your socks and the most exquisite colours you can find. Wearing unusual socks is always a great boost, especially when you're not in the mood for working out. Little touches, such as white socks printed with swaying palm trees, will make you feel energized and look terrific.

▶ TO JAZZ up conservative, straight pants or faded denim jeans, wear glittery, metallic socks in silver, gold, or copper tones. Socks like these combine nicely with classic shoes, such as leather penny or tassle loafers, moccasins, or even leather pumps.

Design Your Own Socks

Permanent-ink magic markers are an easy-to-handle tool for the budding sock artist. Remember to check the label before buying—permanent ink is the only kind of ink that will stand up to repeated washings; other kinds can run onto your other clothes during the wash cycle. Socks that are one hundred percent nylon readily absorb permanent inks; so do one hundred percent cotton sweat socks, tights, or anklets of any weight. Stay away from crocheted or heavily textured cottons, however, as these may not take colour evenly.

Before colouring, make certain the stencil is firmly covering the sock, insuring a precise, sharp image. For extra definition, outline the stenciled design with a black, fine-point permanent marker.

Further tips: You could also make your own stencils by cutting oaktag with an X-Acto knife. Other colouring materials you could use are permanent spray paint, liquid permanent ink, or fabric dye applied with a sable brush. For a truly beautiful pattern, try using a whisk brush dipped in fabric dye. The straw fibers leave an interesting design on thin cottons. You can find whisk brushes in supermarkets and household supply stores.

Create your own freehand designs with permanent-ink magic markers; you may or may not need to work from sketches. Copy your favorite post card or abstract painting. Draw your favorite symbols, animals, or seashells.

▶ FOR ULTRA-VIBRANT socks, dye them at home for pennies. Just be sure that you use one hundred percent cotton socks that have been soaked in hot water before being immersed in the dye. (Soaking the fabric helps it to thoroughly absorb the dye pigment.) Powdered dyes are recommended, since their colours dilute more readily and take to materials more vividly than liquid ones. It's a sensible idea to buy a package of dye remover, too, just in case you miss your desired shade. Just immerse the garment in dye remover, rinse it, and try again.

Remember, any clothing made of one hundred percent cotton can be dyed—including camisoles, petticoats, pantyhose, T-shirts, and sweatpants. Here's how: Wear a pair of thin rubber gloves, unless you don't mind slightly discoloured hands. Line a hand-strainer with a paper towel or coffee filter. Put the dye mix in the liner and hold the strainer under the faucet while you fill a stoppered sink or a plastic tub with very hot water. Stir the water until you see that the dye has dissolved completely. Before you start dyeing, gauge the intensity of the shade with a swatch of white cotton or a white paper towel. (Never use the garment itself as a test material!) Next, immerse your presoaked socks or garment in the sink until it turns several shades darker than you want it to be in the end; it will dry to the shade you desire. After dyeing your socks, dip them into a sink full of cold water with half a cup of vinegar thoroughly mixed into it; this will prevent the colour from fading in subsequent washings. As an added precaution, always wash them in cold water with a mild soap because the high temperature of washing machine water invariably causes hand-dyed garments to run. Rinse them in cold water as well.

For funky, vertically striped socks, get some rubber bands (the thinner the elastic, the narrower the stripe will be) and start tie-dyeing. Beginning at the toe area, wrap a band an inch or so from the toe, then every inch or so on up the sock. Twist each band so that it is tightly secured, and leave about an inch of material between each band. Try dyeing the foot of the sock one colour and the cuff another colour, for added effect.

Do you like to wear socks in all the colours of the rainbow, in every pattern imaginable, socks with special details such as sequins, embroidery, ribbons, or lace? You can quickly and easily design your own at home, for a fraction of what you'd pay in the store for comparably embellished socks or anklets. The first step is to buy 100% cotton, solid-coloured or white socks at a variety or hosiery store; how you intend to decorate them will determine what fabric to choose. Here are a few ideas:

▶ FOR DESIGNING patterned socks, use oaktag or plastic stencils, which can be found at art-supply shops, hardware, and variety stores. Begin by tautly pinning one sock to a sheet of corrugated cardboard or any other thick surface, such as cork. Insert a strip of cardboard inside the sock before colouring to prevent the colours you apply to one side from staining the other.

▶ EMBROIDERED SOCKS can look luxuriously handcrafted, even if you only know one or two stitches. Simple designs such as embroidered polka dots, stars, hearts, eyes, or words can easily be completed in an hour or less. With embroidery, there's no limit to what you can design; use your imagination! Incorporate different qualities of threads for a tapestrylike effect. Metallic threads combined with turquoise, violet, and orange look positively painterly on a pair of plain white socks.

▶ FOR FRINGED effects on the cuffs of your anklets, sew on sequins, pearl beads, ceramic buttons or beads, crystals—anything that your needle and thread can fit through. Or, if you're in love with glitter, scatter sequins over an entire pair of socks, from top to bottom.

▶ SEWING A circlet of lace around the cuffs of your socks gives them a frothy, formal touch. You might also want to sew tiny satin bows on the cuffs to match a black, semiformal outfit.

Besides being made from a comfortable fabric in an attractive design, a bra must define your silhouette with elegance.

Lingerie for On Top

The type of bra you wear should be predicated on the size and shape of your breasts. To prevent your breasts from sagging, always wear bras that provide maximum support, like padded or underwired models. Also, your brassieres should fit exactly! There should never be excess fabric bunched or puckered under your blouse creating an unsightly silhouette. And a bra that is too tight will dig into your flesh at the shoulders or underneath your breasts, causing bulges and discomfort. When you're in the fitting room, try on a sweater or blouse over the bra to make sure it gives you a rounded, natural line.

No matter what your bust size is, if you play a lot of sports or jog, try wearing one of the sports bras on the market. Well-padded with comfortable layers of cotton and spandex, these bras support the pectoral muscles and protect breasts from bouncing. Olga's Christina No-Bounce Sportsbra is especially recommended. Its discreet halter-top design is even suitable for wearing as the top half of your exercise outfit.

Naturally, if your breasts are small, you don't really have to concern yourself with special design features. You can wear stretch cottons, nylons, or silks without worrying about the force of gravity. It's worth noting, however, that underwire bras—without padding—provide subtle uplift for large- and small-breasted women alike. Sheer underwires are especially good for wearing underneath tight-fitting or thin blouses; no seams or textured materials will show through, because sheer underwires don't have any. The bra's fabric is a simple, stretchy synthetic, such as nylon or spandex, and there is a wire at the bottom of the cup.

You can make sure your bra straps are inconspicuous by sewing bra-strap holders into any dresses, tank tops, or other garments with which they might slip into view. For garments that are cut low around the shoulders, armholes, or in front, strapless bras or bandeaus are much more suitable than regular bras. Strapless bras come in padded, unpadded, and underwired versions. Bandeaus are usually made of a thin cotton or synthetic strip of fabric; they are not padded and therefore do not give much support. Bandeaus are ideal, however, for wearing in warm weather or under clingy fabrics.

Indulge in a matching bra and underpants set; top it off with a sinuous dressing gown for intimate allure.

Bodystockings are a nice alternative to mismatched undergarments. They also mold your figure with lightweight comfort.

Essential Underthings

Another valuable—maybe even essential—piece of lingerie to have in your wardrobe is an all-in-one. Cut like a one-piece swimsuit, an all-in-one molds your body attractively; it makes your body look most becoming under delicate or sleekly styled garments. All-in-ones also provide a comfortable and warm solution to winter lingerie needs.

Identical in design to the all-in-one, a teddy is an unconstructed, decorative, and much more glamourous lingerie item. Ruffle- or lace-trimmed teddies add a formal, feminine touch to any outfit you wear. As most teddies are made of fragile fabrics such as silk or rayon, remember to clean them properly after each wearing. If you love the look and feel of a teddy but your funds are limited, a synthetic material such as polyester would be your best buy: It will last longer than silk, and you'll save on dry-cleaning bills. Teddies also make very glamourous sleep- or lounge-wear.

Granted, teddies and all-in-ones are useful and enjoyable to own, but because of their styling, they're totally unsuitable for wearing out to dinner with, for instance, just a jacket and a skirt. The one *de luxe* lingerie article that's designed to be seen—and invariably marks an outfit with romantic sophistication—is the camisole. This old-fashioned garment is a liberated version of what was once called a "bodice." Camisoles came back into vogue when women discovered the unique beauty of vintage lingerie. Now a staple accessory for women who enjoy the alluring detail it adds to any outfit, a camisole can be made of such fabrics as silk or linen and decorated with lace, ribbons, or intricate stitching. More extravagant camisoles are adorned with special touches such as tiny pearls, rhinestones, embroidery, satin bows, or sequins.

A silk camisole trimmed with lace or other decoration will probably cost more than most lingerie items, and if it's an antique one, you might have to pay quite a bit. But because of its special value to your wardrobe, an investment like this is easily justifiable. Besides looking lovely under a classic black pantsuit or a formal silk blouse for evening wear, a camisole can flavor more casual clothes with unexpected glamour. For instance, camisoles peeking from under semitailored blouses, Hawaiian shirts, or faded denim jackets and shirts give you an air of throwaway chic that's perfect for relaxed parties or warm-weather dressing.

Camisoles and teddies are practical undergarments wrapped up in luxurious loungewear. Get one in silk for maximum warmth.

A decorative camisole and slip set can give your total look an invisible boost. You may also want to invest in a mini-length slip for above the knee skirts.

Vintage Undergarments

Few contemporary lingerie designs approximate the look and feel of a garment made from Old World silk, cotton, or brocade. What's more, the exquisite embroidery, lush jacquard prints, and expertly stitched seams, hems, and collars found in antique lingerie qualify them as more than clothes; they're museum pieces, to be worn and cared for with special attention and satisfaction. There are several places you can look for vintage lingerie: Flea markets, used clothing stores, estate sales, and auctions are where you'll find the lowest priced garments; if you can afford to make a bigger investment, then you should scout antique clothing stores.

When you're shopping for vintage undergarments, bear in mind that even if a garment is slightly damaged or yellowed with age, it still may be salvageable. Make minor clothing repairs yourself or go to a tailor and have the garment restitched along its original seams. This shouldn't cost much, and if you bargained for the damaged garment in the first place (as all savvy shoppers do), you've got a rare article of clothing for a very good price. You can revitalize faded cottons or linens by dyeing them in classic lingerie colours such as black, pink, gray, or beige. For a subtly nostalgic hue, many vintage clothiers recommend dyeing faded white garments in a sinkful of tea that has been steeped for ten to fifteen minutes.

The following is a list of vintage garments that can be recycled into your wardrobe as accessories and staples:

▶ MANY VINTAGE long sleeved, short-sleeved, and sleeveless nightgowns can be worn as dresses. Wear an opaque, full slip with matching hose underneath, and you've got a dress that is perfect for summery parties, weddings, or nights on the town. Or, if the nightgown is somewhat sheer, wear a camisole under it with a matching half-slip.

▶ ROBES, DRESSING gowns, and kimonos also can be adapted into dresses by adding an oversized brooch or a coordinated belt or sash. For a more secure closure, sew in hooks and eyes or snaps. Hint: Men's dressing gowns and robes are also worth turning into dresses. If the pattern suits you, then wear it! If it's too large for your frame, think about altering it to fit. Save any leftover fabric and use it for a sash or a scarf.

▶ KIMONOS LOOK dressy and dramatic with coordinated pants or long skirts. Because they are usually made of featherweight fabric, they look best paired with garments of fine textured weaves, such as silk, rayon, linen, or cotton. If you're lucky enough to find a jacquard or print kimono (jacquard is a finely woven, embroidered fabric with an intricate motif, such as Chinese characters or flower blossoms) be sure to team it with a pair of dressy silk pants or a narrow cut skirt that complements the kimono design. If you turn a kimono into a dress, you'll get more wear out of it, and it will be a better investment.

▶ A BED jacket can be restyled into a blouse by adding lace or ribbon trim and sewing closures up the front of the garment. With an opaque slip or camisole peeking out from underneath, it's ready to wear beyond the boudoir.

▶ LAST, BUT not least, are pyjamas in sensuous fabrics such as satin, silk, and rayon. For evening wear, a man-tailored, full-cut pyjama top can be worn as a tunic over a pair of black slacks. With a dressy black belt, you've got a stylish and comfortable outfit, as appropriate for a discotheque as it is for the opera.

▶ TAP PANTS are cut like shorts and sometimes are slit at the sides or have ribboned or lace trims. Comfortable for wearing under loose-fitting pants or skirts in cold weather, they make particularly sexy pyjama bottoms as well.

Vintage lingerie must be treated with special care. Most silk garments should be dry cleaned only. Cotton ones should be washed in mild soap and water. Hang all garments to dry. Between wearings, keep vintage pieces wrapped in tissue paper.

More Essential Lingerie

If you wear dresses or skirts often, your wardrobe won't be complete without either a bra-slip or a regular full-length slip, plus one or two half-slips. Light weight silk or nylon are the best slip fabric choices. Bra-slips are reinforced on top, so they're excellent garments for medium- to large-breasted women. They give any women a seamless silhouette under snugly tailored dresses. Full-length slips are a fashion necessity, for they prevent your skirts and dresses from clinging to your pantyhose. If you wear slit skirts or dresses, be sure to find a slip that matches these discreetly, both in cut and in colour. Beige seems to be the most versatile colour for slips, but your choice should be keyed to *your* wardrobe's colour scheme. Strapless dresses and gowns require a strapless slip to make the garment hang in the most flattering way.

There are lots of updated tap pants available today. You may even be able to find cotton tap pants that come with a matching cotton camisole. Besides cotton, other good fabric choices would be lightweight silk or nylon. Avoid cheap synthetic blends, which invariably cling to your clothing.

Take the time to find lingerie that fits you well in all the right places. Your clothes will look better, and you will feel better and more confident.

Legwear and Lingerie • 47

The all-in-one above, with its low back and scooped armholes, qualifies as a wardrobe staple. Notice the plunging neckline and side on the slip to the left. These design features make it perfect under revealing skirts and dresses.

Television actress Donna Mills wears a pastel coloured, layered bodywear ensemble of mini-shirt, leotard, tights, and leggings, to keep her looking chic during even the most rigourous workout.

High-Tech Bodywear

Along with the recent boom in physical fitness, dancewear such as leotards, unitards, and bodyhose, have become extremely practical and fashionable as lingerie garments. You can now find one hundred percent cotton leotards, and many designs are suitable for wearing under casual jackets or even alone as a shirt. Unitards are essentially leotards with legs; they come in long-sleeved, short-sleeved, and sleeveless models. Some unitards stop at the ankle, and others have stirrups. They are available in a variety of colours and styles in cotton and nylon blends, as well as one hundred percent nylon.

Capezio and Danskin are two of the best dancewear manufacturers; their extensive colour selection and durable designs are available in department stores, dancewear shops, and lingerie boutiques around the world. Flexitard and Carushka are two names to look for in unitards. Although unitards are sometimes expensive, they are worth owning if you take dance or aerobics classes regularly. Many women bodybuilders wear sleeveless unitards for workouts because of the clear view these garments give of the muscles in motion. So, if you're serious about working out, unitards may help inspire you and spur your progress.

Although bodyhose are too fragile for workouts, they're excellent undergarments for sleek-fitting dresses, pants, and blouses. A sort of filmy nylon "undersuit," bodyhose have spaghetti straps and unconstructed busts. The material stretches over the body like pantyhose, and covers the feet in the same manner.

Legwear and lingerie are more than just decorative apparel; they form the foundation of your total look. They make you more comfortable by supporting your muscles and veins during a long day spent on your feet. Given the considerable effect undergarments and legwear have on your appearance and well-being, purchase these items carefully.

Chapter Three:

By now, your basic wardrobe should exemplify simplicity, functionalism, and elegance, and you're well on the way to *Accessory Chic*. It's time for a discussion of jewellery and all its myriad forms.

Most jewellery, except for a watch, is ornamental and nonfunctional; therefore, the choice of style is a highly personal matter. You can either stick to classics like gold, silver, and pearls, or experiment with bolder materials, colours, styles, and textures. Given what these items cost, when questions of real-versus-fake jewellery arise, you may want to heed the advice of New York fashion designer Keni Valenti: "If you want to save money, *versatile* jewellery is much more important than quantity. Less is definitely, *always* more!" Keni is living proof of this maxim; the only piece of jewellery that he wears is a silver, chain-link bracelet from Tiffany & Company. Although it cost him a lot, its classic design is appropriate with dressy, stylized clothing or a T-shirt and jeans. Consider that Keni wears this bracelet twenty-four hours a day, 365 days a year, and his investment was minimal. "Women buy too many clothes, and they usually have a drawerful of mismatched jewellery, also" he says. "The way to avoid this syndrome is by only buying what you *love*, and if that means saving up for a string of cultured pearls, then that's what you should do. They'll last forever, they add a touch of class to daytime and formal clothing, and they simplify your life by being the centerpiece of your accessories."

If you think Keni is overly purist in his approach to accessories, bear in mind that the pieces he designed for Betsey Johnson's 1979 spring collection were fashioned from car parts, household utensils, and hardware. "Anything can be fashion," he says, "it's just how you put it together." Indeed, jewellery made out of unexpected materials can look a lot more *de luxe* and ornamental than it sounds. The Costume Institute of New York's Metropolitan Museum of Art has acquired several of Keni's pieces for its permanent collection.

The spirit of your clothes and the image you wish to present to the world should determine your choice of jewellery. There are literally thousands of pieces, styles, and materials to choose from. Perhaps the most basic piece is a wristwatch, followed by necklaces, earrings, bracelets, and bangles. Some women prefer to buy matching earring-and-necklace sets, but if you're like most, you collect various pieces and coordinate them to suit specific outfits and occasions. An exception to this is rings, since many women wear the same silver, gold, or gemstone rings regardless of their earrings, necklaces, or bracelets.

The type of ring(s) you wear is a highly personal choice, but make sure it coordinates with your other pieces and styles of jewellery. Be careful that the combination of your ring with other jewellery never overpowers you. For example, combining a chunky, molded silver ring with heavy silver bracelets can weigh you down. Conversely, several small rings on each hand looks just as flashy and overdone, especially if the rings are set with gemstones.

Styling Advice

Here are other pointers and added inspiration for coordinating your jewellery:

▶ SINCE YOU probably wear a watch during the day, select *only* those bracelets that are a tasteful accompaniment to your timepiece. When in doubt, wear your watch by itself. Since you don't necessarily need your watch in the evening, wear the bracelets then instead.

▶ WEAR BRACELETS that follow the cuffline of your garment. Avoid those that clump around the cuffs of your sweater, jacket, or blouse. Do, however, wrap bracelets around the cuffs of fabrics such as silk or wool jersey, and also wear bracelets around leather or fabric gloves. If you favor ruffled sleeves, accentuate them by wearing cuff bracelets *above* the ruffles for an old fashioned elegant effect.

▶ ANY NECKLACE you wear should follow the shape of your garment's neckline. Nothing looks worse than a well-cut dress topped with a necklace that violates the contour of its neckline.

▶ NEVER MIX your earthy, ethnic jewellery (amber, cinnabar, turquoise, corals, or seashells) with your more luxurious pieces (pearls, sapphires, or delicate crystals). Mixing different styles of costume jewellery, such as *faux* pearls with rhinestones, usually works, but precious metals and gemstones mixed with basic pieces, such as jade bracelets, are just not appropriate.

A Brief Summary of Specific Jewellery Materials

Generally, jewellery can be divided into precious, semiprecious, period, and costume. Precious jewellery includes real metals, such as gold and silver, cultured pearls, and precious gemstones, such as diamonds, emeralds, rubies, and sapphires. Semiprecious jewellery encompasses gold-plated jewellery and pieces made from substances such as ivory, tiger's-eye, jade, and silver. Examples of period jewellery are Victorian gold bangle bracelets, silver-plated reproductions of ancient Roman pendant necklaces, or 1950s, clip-on enamelled earrings. Costume jewellery is the most affordable style of jewellery, and therefore, the most popular. Faux pearls, imitation gemstones, and gold- and silver-toned chains and earrings are but a few examples. Here are detailed descriptions of all these types of jewellery and more.

Pearls

There are three types of pearls—natural, cultured, and imitation (also called faux pearls). Naturally formed Oriental pearls are the most lustrous and beautiful pearls in the world; they're also quite rare, and therefore expensive. Although cultured pearls are cultivated by man, they're also on the expensive side. If you can't afford them, there are several brands of imitation pearls. Jewelers recommend Majorica pearls as the highest quality imitations; every strand is guaranteed to last for at least ten years.

When buying any kind of pearls, make sure they are securely strung and knotted between each pearl. Also, the clasp must be easy to operate and should be decorative, but not so ornate that it appears gaudy. The best way to choose a string of faux pearls is to go to a jeweler and ask to see their most expensive, highest quality imitation strand. Work your way down from there until you find a strand that suits both your sense of quality and your budget.

*Pearls are the **ne plus ultra** of jewellery. Whether they are real, artful fakes, or even obvious fakes, pearls add romantic polish to whatever you wear.*

Caring for Pearls

To test a string of pearls for authenticity, rub the pearls over your teeth. If they grate, they are real; if they feel smooth, they are imitations. Additionally, genuine pearls will feel cooler to the touch than fake ones.

Leave cultured pearls out on your dresser when you're not wearing them so they can "breathe." Airing them will deepen their lustre. Because pearls absorb the natural oils in your skin, they will also grow more lustrous with each wearing. Never spray perfume on your pearls; this will dull their surface.

Consider eye colour, skin tone, and hair colour when choosing gemstone jewellery.

Precious and Semiprecious Gemstones

With so many beautifully hued precious and semiprecious gems in existence, there are sure to be a few that will both appeal to your colour sense and enhance your wardrobe. It's definitely worth sinking some money into one piece of gemstone jewellery—earrings, a pendant, or a pin—that will go with all of your outfits and complement the other jewellery you wear often, such as a string of pearls or a gold chain.

Here is a list of precious and semiprecious gems that you should consider investing in:

PRECIOUS GEMSTONES

PERIDOT: spring green.

AMETHYST: light lavender to deep purple.

BLUE TOPAZ: ice blue.

AQUAMARINE: a white blue, paler than blue topaz.

CITRINE: bright orange.

DIAMOND: sparkling white.

RUBY: very deep red.

EMERALD: rich green.

ONYX: black and shiny, also a deep, rich blue.

SAPPHIRE: glittering dark blue.

OPAL: milky white, with veins of pink, red, blue, and lavender. Opals, which are iridescent, change depending on the light conditions.

JADE: palest green to celadon to seagreen to black.

SEMIPRECIOUS GEMSTONES

ZIRCON: a synthetic, diamondlike stone that is often undetectable as an imitation. Zircons cost appreciably less than diamonds, though they are not low-priced.

IVORY: creamy white to beige. Ivory is carved and otherwise fashioned from the tusks of animals.

EBONY: brown-black, blue-black, or darkest black. Ebony is a highly polished wood that resembles stone.

SODALITE: blue-black stone.

LAPIS LAZULI: midnight blue or dark turquoise stone.

CORAL: creamy white to pink, orangy red to blood red, green to black.

HEMATITE: pearly gray.

ROSE QUARTZ: frosted pink to light lavender.

CRYSTAL: all colours. Some crystals are more prismatic than others.

TIGER'S-EYE: a marbled mixture of gold and rich brown.

AMBER: waxy yellow to orange and red to brown-black.

MOTHER-OF-PEARL: derived from abalone or other lustrous seashells, mother-of-pearl is similar to opal, but very natural looking.

CINNABAR: red to vermillion. Made from tree resins, it is often carved.

Gold

Any piece of gold jewellery is a fine investment that will coordinate with every outfit you wear, as well as dress up your total look. When shopping for gold jewellery, always look for a stamped karat measure on the clasp; for example, 14k or 18k. This indicates how much gold the piece contains and thus, whether the price being asked is a reasonable one. Gold is measured on a scale comprising twenty-four units; a bracelet stamped 12k means that it is fifty percent pure gold, and fifty percent metal alloy. The more gold a piece contains, the more easily it will scratch, dent, or bend under rough handling. If you want to get maximum wear out of your gold jewellery, buy only fourteen-karat or eighteen-karat pieces.

When wearing gold or any other precious metals, take care to keep your overall look tasteful and discreet. Besides drawing too much attention to yourself on the street, wearing an abundance of gold jewellery might backfire by creating the impression that you're wearing costume pieces.

Caring for Gold Jewellery

Always remove gold pieces before exercising or doing any other kind of physical work. Polish gold often with a jeweler's cloth treated with chemicals especially for that purpose. These cloths are available at most jewellery shops, as well as at crafts stores. Keep your gold jewellery in a flannel bag or cotton-lined box to prevent it from tarnishing.

GOLD SUBSTITUTES

If you want more dash than you have cash, the next best thing to gold is either brass or gold-plated jewellery. Specifically, hammered brass is attractive, stylish, and relatively inexpensive. Brass chokers, bracelets, earrings, and pendants can be found at most department stores and in many boutiques.

> ### Caring for Brass
>
> Keep brass jewellery shiny and bright by polishing periodically with brass cleaner and a flannel cloth. You can find brass polish in supermarkets and household supply stores.

It is advisable to choose your gold-plated jewellery from established jewellery manufacturers, such as Christian Dior, and other manufacturers that sell their lines through department stores and specialty shops. These companies produce a superior product; whatever your purchase, it will last you years and years. In general, stay away from gold-plated jewellery sold on the street or in dime stores. You really won't know what you're paying for (even if it is cheap), and venues like these usually don't have customer-service departments for you to write with your complaints. The same rule applies to catalogues that sell gold-plated jewellery—or any other kind, for that matter. Unless it's a reputable company, store, or manufacturer, don't send your money off for questionable goods. You may wind up less than pleased with your purchase and find it impossible to get a refund.

SILVER

Certain styles of silver, copper, or bronze jewellery can be even more expensive than eighteen-karat gold. Silver and turquoise American Indian pieces are a prime example. Although the exquisite craftsmanship of jewellery like this partially justifies the cost, a turquoise and silver squash blossom necklace can be very expensive, depending on the intricacy of the design and the age of the piece. On the other hand, there are thousands of silver jewellery styles that are reasonably priced and very useful for achieving a well-appointed total look. Since sterling silver is more affordable than real gold, it makes good wardrobe sense to have at least one sterling bracelet, necklace, or pair of earrings. Look for the sterling silver stamp on the clasp before buying.

> ### Caring for Silver
>
> To keep your silver pieces looking their brightest, polish them with silver polish and a flannel cloth or, if you prefer, a jeweler's cloth. Never use an abradant cleanser on your jewellery; this will surely scratch and dull the surface.

COPPER AND BRONZE

The colour and sheen of copper and bronze jewellery make it especially suitable with wardrobes that favor earth-tones, darker primary colours, ethnic designs such as Indian, African, and Asian prints, or hand-dyed, handwoven clothing. If you think copper and bronze are second-class metals, you will be surprised to find out that they are often part of a high-fashion look these days. A quick glance through any fashion magazine will reveal everything from hammered bronze necklaces with wooden beads to antique copper-and-turquoise pendants and high-tech, sculptural necklaces in geometric shapes studded with precious gemstones. Innovative jewellery boutiques and galleries regularly feature beautifully handcrafted contemporary jewellery in copper and bronze, pieces that are collector's items. Of course, buying jewellery made by artisans is beyond most women's means, but if distinctive jewellery is important to you, this is one route to consider.

For more affordable copper and bronze jewellery, any department store will have a good selection. Look for naturalistic designs such as leaf shapes, big-beaded pendants, wide-collar chokers, and delicate chains that can be worn singly or together. Vintage copper and bronze jewellery is *the* perfect accessory for vintage clothing. Look in antique stores, and flea markets, and whenever possible, buy earrings and bracelets that match the necklaces you find. Take good care of your antique jewellery combinations with copper or bronze polish and a flannel cloth. Also, if the necklace you picked up at a flea market is broken or very fragile, be sure to repair it or strengthen it before you wear it.

CRYSTALS

There are a few low-cost alternatives to sterling silver jewellery that you may not have considered before—crystals, for instance. There are many types of crystals, the most popular being smooth beads, faceted glass, and geometrically shaped, painted-lead prismatic beads. Crystals come in many different colours and, when strung on silver-tone chains or set in silver-tone earring studs, their natural beauty rivals that of any expensive piece of sterling silver jewellery.

Ilene Kaufman Designs, based in New York and distributed worldwide, is an avant-garde jewellery company that features exquisite costume silver and crystal pieces, most of which are made from prismatic, Austrian crystals. "The main advantage of crystals is that they mix well with all sorts of precious and semiprecious stones; you can even com-

This elegant, jet-black crystal earring and necklace duo from Ilene Kaufman Designs is a smashing update of nostalgic jewellery styles and substances. In a more minimal, modern mode, the silver pieces above are classic accessories for any occasion.

Enhance your total look with distinctively crafted jewellery pieces, and you'll never be less than well-dressed.

bine pearl jewellery with crystal pieces, Ilene explains. "The other points that crystals have in their favor apply to all women: They make the eyes sparkle and brighten up the face, while flattering all complexions and hair colours.

PERIOD JEWELLERY

The distinctive designs and details of period jewellery make it well-worth considering for your accessories collection. Whether authentic or reproductions, period bracelets, earrings, necklaces, and rings will add flair to both casual and dressy outfits and set you apart from the crowd. Styles include ancient Greek and Roman, Byzantine, Victorian, art nouveau, and art deco. Reproductions of period jewellery designs can be found in most museum shops, such as the Metropolitan Museum of Art in New York or the British Museum in London.

RHINESTONES

Rhinestone jewellery has been a fashion staple for most of the twentieth century. Though they lack the mystique of diamonds, rhinestones dress up an outfit with sparkling flair. There are many coloured rhinestones besides the traditional whites; pink, emerald, ruby, and sapphire are just a few. Since rhinestones are relatively inexpensive, you can afford to wear several different pieces at the same time, if that's your style. Most department stores and boutiques carry a large selection in a price range of budget to moderately expensive. Flea markets and dime stores also are veritable treasure troves of faux gemstone or "paste" jewellery.

PLASTIC JEWELRY

It is unarguable that most plastic jewellery falls short of the standards of *Accessory Chic*. This does not mean that you should rule out plastics altogether, though. It is possible to find exceptionally well-designed, high-quality plastic jewellery in boutiques or department stores, at some very high prices. Plastic *lalique* looks lovely by itself and coordinates nicely with silver and pearls or gold and various gemstones. For another approach, keep an eye out for vintage forties and fifties plastic jewellery at flea markets or used clothing boutiques.

Watches

Now that you've got a general idea of the many materials to choose from, it's time to discuss particular jewellery pieces, beginning with your timepiece.

The choice of a wristwatch is a very personal decision. Although it is impossible to dictate which style is most suitable for a particular woman's wardrobe or taste level, you have three basic categories to choose from: classic, sporty, and elegant. Classic watches look correct with office wardrobes, casual wear, and dressier outfits; naturally, they look best when teamed with classic jewellery. Sporty watches include everything from pink plastic wristwatches to digital ones that time your laps as you swim or jog. Elegant watches are especially decorative and styled primarily for evening wear. Since a watch is the most essential piece of jewellery that you'll ever own, it's worth choosing carefully and saving your money to buy one that comes with a warranty for repairs. A watch is a finely tuned machine; if you care for it responsibly, it should last a lifetime.

If versatility is what you want from a watch, then go for a style like the "tank" watch, designed by the famous French jeweler, Cartier. With a thin rectangular face, Roman numerals, and no second hand, the tank watch is a study in simplicity and is flattering to any wrist. A genuine Cartier tank watch is very expensive, but most de-

The clean design and affordable price of Swatch watches have made them de rigeur *timepieces all over the world.*

partment stores and jewelers offer imitations that are more reasonable. If you need an all-purpose watch, as appropriate for the office as for evening, consider buying a tank watch with a black face, gold Roman numerals, and a black lizard-skin band.

Other classic styles include any watch with a round, oval, or octagonal face and cleanly styled or Roman numerals. The choice between a leather or lizard-skin band is up to you. Lizard skin is more expensive, but it's also a little more chic. One way to get a great watch for a relatively low price is to buy a classic Timex watch and dress it up with a beautiful lizard band. The watch is not expensive, but the look will be much more distinguished than the cost would suggest.

In the last decade, digital watches have become popular timepieces because they are reasonably priced and have multiple functions. A Casio sportswatch tells you the time and date and can be programmed to ring an alarm to wake you up in the morning or set to sound every hour. Two kinds of stopwatches are built into a Casio—one that records time in minutes, seconds, and hundredths of seconds and another that records it in seconds, minutes, and hours. Look for a digital watch that is both water-resistant and shockproof, and of course, get one that comes with a warranty. Although digital watches such as Casios have plastic-sprocketed bands that are rather boring to look at they hold up well to perspiration and immersion in water.

Perhaps you prefer a more decorative sporty watch. Timex and Bradley both have cartoon-character watches that are colourful, inexpensive, and highly amusing. Of course, the Mickey Mouse watch will always be available around the world and be worn by children from ages four to ninety-four. For cheap chic, nothing beats a Mickey Mouse watch worn with a black lizard-skin band. There are also many watches on the market with boldly detailed graphics across the faces. Trocadero, a San Francisco-based jewellery company, makes watches with everything from penguins to palm trees to Marilyn Monroe as a backdrop for the hands of time. These watches are available at most department stores and boutiques around the world.

If you have a taste for modern simplicity, then investigate the Swiss line of Swatches. They are very attractive, with a classic, round-faced shape and a clean line in the watchband. Swatches are made completely of plastic and are available in department stores and boutiques around the world. The specific designs range from conventional, numbered faces to futuristic, numberless hands against a pure black backdrop. Swatch also makes one of the more unusual timepieces on the market—pastel, scented wristwatches. The watchbands are aromatically treated to smell like banana, raspberry, and mint. Accordingly, they come in pastel yellow, pink, and green.

Depending on your income and the type of formal clothes you wear, you might want to consider investing in a vintage wristwatch, or a decorative modern one with a sterling silver or gold band. Or, a watch bracelet might be the perfect accessory for lending an elegant, finishing touch to your total look. Instead of conventional leather straps, watch bracelets have decorative chains or bands that encircle the wrist. The more elaborate models have jewelled clasps, and can therefore be easily coordinated with earrings, necklaces, and bracelets.

New York's Museum of Modern Art sells an assortment of high-tech jewellery and other accessories.

Necklaces

Because of the added dimension they bring to your wardrobe, necklaces are one of the most useful accessories you can own. Whether you spruce up a plain neckline with a strand of pearls or wear a gold chain to match metallic earrings, a necklace can be one of the key elements of your total look. And, no matter if your taste runs to classic pieces, ethnic styles, or drop-dead chic gold and gemstones, there are many style possibilities to try within each category. Perhaps it's best to begin with a discussion of classic necklace styles.

DIFFERENT PEARLY LOOKS

Diamonds may be a girl's best friend, but unless you're a gold digger, a string of pearls makes a much more practical, classic and worthwhile investment. Pearls add understated elegance to any blazer or suit you wear; they make a dress into an *evening* dress; they add lustre to monochromatic outfits that desperately need livening up.

If you do go ahead and invest in a string of cultured pearls, don't hesitate to mix them with fakes when you're dressing for a festive, bejewelled look. Since pearls come in a variety of strand-lengths and numerous colours such as gray, pink, and black, there are unlimited ways you can wear them. Here are some suggestions:

▶ WEAR ONE long strand of pearls, knotted in the middle or just below the throat.

▶ WEAR SEVERAL strands of gray, pink, and black pearls in different lengths. One could be a choker, the other a longer strand, the last a long strand knotted in the middle, near your waistline. If you're uncomfortable wearing so many different shades, stick with all-white pearls.

▶ WEAR A choker around your neck, plus one or more long strands.

▶ WEAR A long strand of pearls wrapped a couple of times as a choker, or wrap it around your wrist as a bracelet.

▶ WEAR A pearl necklace with the jewelled clasp positioned so it shows in front.

Another fashionable plus to pearl necklaces is that they coordinate so easily with other jewellery. Pearls mix with gold, silver, brass, and crystals, as well as many other precious and semiprecious materials. But if simplicity's your thing, then all you need for a classic jewellery ensemble is a pair of pearl studs or hanging teardrop earrings, plus a few pearl bangles or a pearl cuff bracelet. These acces-

Even gold-plated jewellery will add a murmur of opulence to your image.

sories will take you through evening engagements for the next couple of decades and by then, you'll have saved up enough money for diamonds.

Gold necklaces

An eighteen-karat gold chain is one of the most versatile, high-quality accessories that you'll ever own. The most versatile length is forty centimeters (sixteen inches), which falls just on the collarbone and complements most necklines. Many women wear their gold necklaces all the time, accessorizing with other pieces.

To get you thinking along the right lines, here are some specifics for choosing real and gold-plated necklace styles. You can even mix real gold chains with imitation ones or with other necklace styles. Whatever styles you combine, however, be sure that the proportions mix harmoniously. You want to avoid an overdone "top heavy" look, so when in doubt, wear only one necklace.

▶ TRY A gold-plated chain with imitation pearls strung on it. Wear this with a string of real or imitation pearls. Combine them with real gold or gold-toned earrings, bracelets, and rings.

▶ GOLD-PLATED CHAINS braided with white or black enamel chains echo the colour of a black suit or white blouse. Necklaces styled this way look most appropriate for the office or for semiformal occasions: they're too "serious" for most evening looks.

▶ REAL GOLD chains look great mixed with gold-plated necklaces set with pearls, rhine-

stones, or semiprecious gems. For instance, try mixing an eighteen-karat gold chain with a gold-plated necklace that has a faux pearl or rhinestone pendant on it. The gold-plated chain should be a little longer than the eighteen-karat chain.

▶ REAL GOLD or gold-tone chains with crystal, ivory, or other semiprecious stones can be worn to match specific colours in your wardrobe, such as a gold-plated necklace with rose quartz beads to complement a lavender sweater. Chains with glass, plastic, or lucite beads can also look quite stylish and suitable for day and evening wear.

▶ ADD CHARMS to a gold chain. There are even many gold charms you can find that are reasonably priced. If you like to mix metals, then silver charms or brass cloisonné beads are possible ornaments for a gold chain. If you're feeling funky, anything from a stray earring or pin to a Crackerjack toy can be attached to a chain. Antique shops and flea markets are a great source for offbeat pendant materials. Use your imagination.

Brass necklaces

For a summery or ethnic look, nothing is better than a necklace of big brass beads strung on a thin leather thong. Brass necklaces are usually wide and bold, not delicate, so emphasize them with a wristful of thin brass bangles. Or try a wide brass cuff enamelled with a floral, cloisonné design. Naturally, brass earrings are next. Yours could be hammered hoops or just small studs; sometimes a flash of brass at the ear looks better than a bigger piece of jewellery.

Remember that your necklace should complement the neckline of your dress, blouse, or sweater.

SILVER OPTIONS

If you have a sterling silver chain, accessorize it with sterling silver charms, for they're relatively inexpensive and available in every imaginable style and substance. From precious gemstones to Victorian period sterling lockets to modern, geometric designs, you can create a dozen different necklace looks with just a sterling chain and a handful of charms. Wear the charms singly or a couple together on the chain. The only rule is to choose charms in designs and hues that work in concert with the dominant styles and colours of your wardrobe.

Here are some other ways to wear sterling silver chains:

▶ WEAR A sterling or silver-tone necklace, adorned with turquoise or red coral beads that is slightly longer than your chain. Wear matching turquoise or coral earrings.

▶ ADD SPARKLE to a sterling chain by wearing it with a long strand of rhinestones set in silver-tone metal.

SHINE WITH RHINESTONES

Add the most dazzle to nighttime dressing by wearing two or three rhinestone necklaces in different gemstone colours. Examples include an amethyst rhinestone choker and a strand of sapphire rhinestones. Or wear two narrow, white rhinestone chokers at once. Look for rhinestone necklaces that have decorative clasps, for details like these make your jewellery all the more special.

PLASTIC NECKLACES AND PENDANTS

Plastic simulations of other substances can be remarkably successful. Jade, coral, crystal, mother-of-pearl, and marble are but a few natural materials that look quite attractive in plastic imitation. Whether you wear beaded plastic necklaces or ones strung with

Biba Schutz Designs' New Wave amulets are kicky costume pieces, perfect for party wear.

plastic pendants or charms, such colourful costume pieces liven up casual dresses and other outfits, especially in the warmer months when more relaxed fashions are in vogue. When wearing plastic jewellery, however, let common sense be your guide. For instance, it's better to wear no jewellery at all than to wear an obviously inexpensive, faux ivory necklace with an elegantly tailored linen suit. Not only will the necklace clash with the suit, but you'll feel uncomfortable. Perhaps a better choice for these clothes would be a string of heavy, translucent faux crystal beads. The clear beads will pick up the colour of your garment and harmonize with it, pulling your look together.

Dress for excess with inspired earring accessorizing. Play up the colour and texture of your clothes by sporting posh ear gear.

Earrings

As you already know, the jewellery you wear should be chosen to some extent on the basis of your face shape and overall bone structure. This rule holds especially true when selecting earrings. If your face is round and full, chunky or wide earrings will only accentuate this. Try drop pendant earrings or long, dangling ones instead to add a slimming proportion to your features. Conversely, women with squarish, angular features can soften their look with large pearl cluster studs or round, gemstone clip-ons. Oversized earrings can also deflect attention from a large bustline or an excessively long neck.

The following chart lists classic and more adventurous earring styles, with suggestions for different types of necklaces to coordinate them with. Use these suggestions as a departure point for coordinating all of your other different pieces of jewellery as well.

EARRINGS	NECKLACES
Gold studs	Gold chains or pearls; gold chains with gemstone beads; gold chains with rhinestones.
Pearl studs	Silver or gold chains; pearl necklaces or choker; ivory beads; coral, rose quartz, or crystals.
Silver studs	Silver and/or turquoise chains; pearls, rhinestones, crystals, *lalique*, faux gemstones, ivory, rose quartz, onyx, or black plastic.
Precious or semiprecious gemstones	Matching or contrasting faux gemstones; rhinestones; pearls; gold and silver chains.
Teardrop-shaped pearls, silver, gold, etc.	Rhinestones; matching silver, gold or pearl necklaces with pendants of gold or silver; crystals.
Gold or silver hoops	Gold or silver charms on gold or sterling chains; pearls; gold beads; silver chains with colourful stones or beads.
Art deco drop earrings studded with rhinestones	Matching period chains with pendants; pearls; crystals; rhinestones; glass beads.
Copper or bronze pendant earrings	Wood beads; copper or bronze chokers; rose quartz beads or pendants; tiger's-eye charms or beads.
Seashell; mother-of-pearl	Jade pendant or imitation jade beads; strand of tiny seashells or silver or gold seashell charms.
Geometric-shaped studs or pendant earrings.	Coordinated necklaces in similar or contrasting shapes.

Jewellery • 65

All of the pieces on this page have an eternal look to them. If you want to get long-term wear out of your jewellery, choose styles that are timeless.

If you are tired of the way your earrings look, or if you have lost one of a pair, try wearing a single earring for a fresh, asymmetrical look.

Other Ear Accessories

Other ear jewellery, such as ear cuffs, are also fun to include in your collection. Ear cuffs, which wrap around the outside of your ear, are one of the oldest forms of adornment. They were worn by ancient Egyptian men and women, as well as by native American Indians. Ear cuffs are back in style today in narrow, delicate designs of hammered silver, brass, and gold; they also come in space-age metals, such as titanium, which happens to be hypo-allergenic. Other popular designs include bands studded with gemstones or cuffs that have dangling, charm-studded chains attached.

Considerations of style and proportion are essential when choosing an ear cuff, especially if you're planning to wear earrings with it. After all, you want the pieces of the ensemble to be in scale with one another. Too much decor hanging from your ears will make you resemble a jewellery rack, and if you're wearing a necklace besides, you want to avoid a gaudy, cluttered look. Here are a few specific examples of appropriate ear cuff-and-earring combinations:

▶ COMPLEMENT A hammered-silver ear cuff with tiny, turquoise stud earrings set in silver. Wear a sterling silver chain around your neck.

▶ EMPHASIZE THE texture and sheen of a hammered, fourteen-karat gold ear cuff with tiny, eighteen-karat gold hoop earrings. Wear these with any type of gold chain or, if you prefer, a string of pearls.

▶ ECHO THE rich colours of a sky blue and violet titanium ear cuff with pendant earrings also made of blue and violet titanium. The earrings could be dangling pendants or small, triangle-shaped shields that hang from titanium ear wires. Wear a necklace that picks up the colours of your earrings and cuffs—for example, a silver chain with an amethyst or rose quartz pendant, or a strand of frosted purple plastic beads.

Pierced versus Clip-on Earrings

It wasn't long ago that in many places pierced ears were considered vulgar, barbaric, and a little too racy for a proper young lady. Time and fashion have helped erase this Puritan attitude, yet there are still many women who prefer clip-on earrings for various reasons. For example, some women have little desire to wear earrings except for formal occasions, and since these may occur only two or three times a year, clip-ons are the most practical earrings for them. Other women simply feel uncomfortable about marring their ears with tiny holes, and clip-ons are a less drastic change than pierced ears. Feeling comfortable in what you wear is the key to looking good, so decide whether to pierce or not to pierce on the basis of which style will make you feel most comfortable.

The ear-piercing procedure is relatively painless, inexpensive, and quick (it's over in a few seconds). Even if you wear the same pair of eighteen-karat gold posts your whole life, you'll always be chicly attired in a classic jewellery look. In this respect, pierced ears are eminently more convenient. The one drawback to wearing pierced earrings over many years is that this often causes sagging earlobes, especially if you wear a lot of heavy, pendant earrings. On the other hand, clip-ons have clasps that sometimes make them unbearably uncomfortable after a few hours of wear. They're also relatively easy to lose when you're pulling a sweater over your head, removing your coat, or rushing down a crowded street. Another disadvantage to clip-ons is that they are often difficult to place symmetrically on each ear to achieve a balanced look.

One thing to watch for with pierced earrings is the quality of the wires or posts you

68 • Accessory Chic

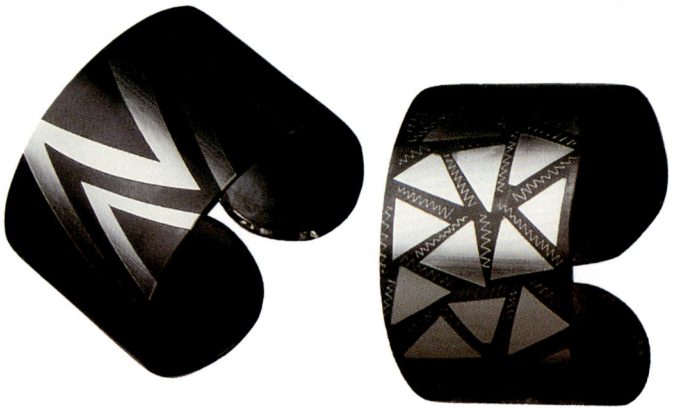

The comic book heroine Wonder Woman wore wrist cuffs imbued with magical properties. Stock up on these bold bracelets; they'll add heroic dash to modern Amazons, as well.

wear. Many people are allergic to certain metals, such as copper, silver, or various other impure alloys, so keep this in mind when you select your earrings. For instance, if you've worn silver jewellery and your skin turns it black, silver posts or wires will undoubtedly infect your ears. If you are wearing a pair of pierced earrings that make your lobes feel irritated and/or warm, this is a sign that your body is reacting against this metal. Take them off immediately and swab the front and back of each ear with rubbing alcohol or another astringent. Surgical steel, fourteen-karat gold, and titanium are the least irritating metals for those with sensitive skin.

Whether or not you wear pierced earrings, keep this in mind when you shop for earrings: If the particular pair you're looking at is a style inappropriate for your ears, you can have them converted to the necessary form. The conversion process is simple and inexpensive, and most jewelers will be glad to do it for you.

At the height of earring style are talented beauties Shirley MacLaine and Marisa Berenson; they both have three pierced holes in one ear and just one pierced hole in the other. You may want to consider this kind of look, especially if you have short hair or wear your hair swept up. A series of pierced holes also suits women who restrict themselves to wearing tiny studs or otherwise delicate jewellery; they can wear lots of colour on their ears without looking excessively accessorized.

With several holes, you can coordinate your earrings in all kinds of interesting ways, such as:

▶ WEAR LONG, dangling pearl earrings in both ears and two faux or real pearl studs in the other.

▶ WEAR ONE long faux onyx earring in one ear and a pearl, a rhinestone, and a silver stud in the other.

▶ WEAR A mix of gold, silver, and pearl studs that are stylistically and proportionately correct for each other.

▶ WEAR A mix of gemstone studs, such as amethyst, sapphire, and diamond, with a tiny gold hoop in the other ear.

Bracelets, Bangles, Bands, and Cuffs

When choosing bracelets, use your wrist size and your watch-style as your primary guides. If your bones are of average or larger width, for example, you can wear virtually all styles, as long as the bracelets are in suitable proportion to your earrings, necklaces, rings, and watches. Women who are particularly fine-boned look best in thinner bracelets or narrow-to-medium-width cuffs. If you have very fine bones, however, you may want to eschew bracelets altogether; a simply designed wristwatch on one arm and a ring or two on the hands are often the appropriate choices for those with small frames. Bracelets can be a particularly tricky accessory in that they're easy to misjudge, so if you think you're wearing the wrong style of bracelet, or perhaps too many of them, take them off!

Just as with your necklaces and earrings, your daytime bracelets should be stylistically appropriate for your professional environment. Choose them in designs that allow freedom of movement. Anything that is too wide, charm-laden, or clanking could undermine your appearance and your performance. You want to project an image of professionalism to your colleagues and superiors, and one of the best ways to botch your success is with indiscreet jewels. A chart of various bracelet looks for casual wear, for office wear, and for evening wear is provided below, but first, here are a few words of advice on which kind of bracelets are suitable for specific situations:

▶ WHEN DRESSING for casual situations, choose more adventurously styled jewellery, such as wide, rounded wooden bracelets that are hand-painted in a colourful, graffiti design. Flea market and vintage bracelets that are chunky, glittery, perhaps a little on the kitschy side—these are for having fun with your look.

▶ ACCESSORIZING YOUR work wardrobe is another story; your bracelets should be subtly styled, but not so dressy as to attract undue attention. For instance, wear a plastic imitation ebony cuff with a black pinstriped suit, or an eighteen-karat gold bangle with a cream-coloured sweater and a gray flannel skirt. The only rule is that your bracelets must contribute to your professional total look.

▶ EVENING DRESSING usually equals elegance, so this is when you wear your real, luxurious jewellery or your most festive and outrageous costume pearls, rhinestones, and crystals. Let the specific nature of the occasion determine how bejewelled you choose to appear. For instance, you may feel comfortable wearing an elaborate crystal bracelet with a little black dress to the ballet, but if you're going to a friend's cocktail party, it may be a bit too dressy.

A basic sportswear look: sunglasses, earrings, and a cuff bracelet.

Casual bracelets

With gold and gold-toned jewellery:

▶ WRAP A favorite necklace around your wrist; it may look better as a bracelet.

▶ MIX GOLD and silver bangles for a pretty metallic contrast.

▶ TRY CRYSTAL, glass, or plastic beaded bracelets.

▶ WEAR A wide brass bangle or cuff.

With silver and silver-toned jewellery, try:

▶ RHINESTONES SET in silver-tone metal.

▶ A DOZEN skinny silver bangles.

▶ AN IMITATION pearl bracelet with a silver clasp.

▶ A SILVER I.D. bracelet.

With various colours and styles of jewellery, match:

▶ BLACK ELEPHANT hair wristlets.

▶ A BRACELET of tiny seashells or coloured seeds.

▶ PLASTIC, IMITATION jade, ivory, tiger's eye or cinnabar bangles.

▶ BEVELLED GLASS bangles.

▶ PLASTIC, IMITATION *lalique* bangles.

Office wear bracelets

With gold and gold-toned jewellery:

▶ A THIN eighteen-karat gold wristlet.

▶ A NARROW, gold-filled bangle bracelet.

▶ A GOLD link wristlet.

▶ A HAMMERED-GOLD cuff bracelet.

▶ A GOLD beaded bracelet interspersed with semiprecious stones.

With silver and silver-toned jewellery:

▶ A SCULPTED sterling cuff.

▶ TWO STERLING bangles.

▶ AN ONYX and silver bangle.

▶ AN INLAID SILVER and mother-of-pearl bangle.

▶ SILVER BEADS with semiprecious stones or interesting and whimsical charms.

With various kinds of jewellery, one or two bracelets in any of these materials might be appropriate:

▶ GREEN OR black jade.

▶ CORAL OR ivory, worn with a cinnabar bangle.

▶ WOOD INLAID with brass or copper.

▶ TORTOISE SHELL

▶ CLEAR OR coloured lucite bangles.

Evening wear bracelets

With gold and gold-toned jewellery:

▶ WEAR A gold-mesh cuff on one arm; several engraved gold or gold-toned bangles on the other.

▶ WEAR AN armful of pearl bracelets: a two-strand white pearl wristlet with a decorative clasp, plus a pink pearl bracelet. (Choose pearl bangles in several different colours to match your evening outfits.)

▶ WEAR GOLD-TONED metal and rhinestone bracelets on one arm, plus a gold-toned bracelet with faceted semiprecious or faux stones on the other.

▶ ENHANCE THE look of a dressy gold-tone or real gold watch on one wrist with a thin gold chain around the other.

With silver and silver-tone jewellery, try:

▶ A SILVER and turquoise cuff on each wrist.

▶ SILVER BANGLES alternated with ivory bangles.

▶ SILVER-TONED BRACELETS with rhinestones; you can add pearl bracelets with silver-toned clasps to these.

▶ SILVER AND crystal bracelets mixed with those of semiprecious or faux stones.

▶ VINTAGE SILVER bracelets in varying styles: engraved bangles, beaded bracelets, or charm bracelets.

Hair Ornaments and Cufflinks

A jewelled hair comb or a pair of colourful gemstone cuff links can add a delightful touch of class to many outfits. While you wouldn't want to include flashy combs, barrettes, or cuff links in your work wardrobe, accessories like these are perfectly suited for evening clothes and semiformal leisure outfits. Department stores and boutiques are the best places to find a wide selection of silver, gold, and costume material combs and barrettes. As for cuff links, look in vintage jewellery stores, flea markets, and department stores. Because most women wear button-cuff blouses, it's rare that you'll find cuff links at the women's jewellery counter. Visit the men's and boy's shops in department stores, instead.

Decorative hair combs are the crowning accessory for long-haired fashion mavins.

For Your Feet

CHAPTER FOUR:

Ancient Chinese acupuncturists determined that the foot is one of the major nerve centers of the body. Because your feet are absolutely essential for carrying you through life but are extremely delicate, they deserve only the best in footwear. Ill-fitting or poor-quality shoes can lead to blisters, corns, bunions, ingrown toenails, and other long-term ailments. Also, the wrong pair of shoes can negatively affect your appearance, health, and mood. So be discriminating when shopping for shoes. And after you've bought them, keep shoes and boots in good repair and looking their best to keep you looking and feeling *your* best.

High Quality Footwear

Here are some design specifics to guide you when choosing high-quality, durable shoes and boots for your particular foot size and shape:

▶ THE MOST important design feature of a shoe is probably the last. The last is a wooden or metal model of the human foot on which shoes or boots are shaped; it then becomes the form of the shoe that supports your entire foot. Manufacturers' lasts vary in shape, design, length, and width. When you find a line of footwear with a last that is comfortable for you, stay with it! If you can't always afford to pay the full retail price, keep an eye out for these shoes on sale; you'll know what you're getting for your money, and you won't be uncomfortable.

▶ THE VAMP is the portion of the shoe or boot that covers the instep of the shoe, the "upper." The importance of having a well-fitting vamp cannot be stressed enough. Think about it: If you buy a pair of great-looking shoes that are too tight across the toes, then you've just paved the way for sore feet and wasted your money. Then again, it is possible to have the shoes stretched by a shoemaker, but sometimes not sufficiently to make room for your toes.

▶ THE INSOLE is the material lining the bottom of the inside of the shoe. As your foot rests on the insole, it's very important that it be properly adhered to the bottom of the shoe and comfortable for you to walk on. Fine leather insoles are preferable, for they absorb perspiration, let your feet breath, and support your feet better than thick leather or synthetic ones.

▶ THE WELT is a strip of leather sewn between the outer sole of a shoe and the edges of its insole and upper. These layers are held together by glue, stitching, or stapling. Shoes with stitched welts are most durable; they resist damage from extended wear and rain better than shoes with glued welts, which tend to come apart rather easily. Stapled welts are poor quality construction; avoid them. Evening shoes or dressier shoes usually have glued welts, for they make a shoe look slimmer and more delicate. Keep this in mind before wearing them out in the rain.

If you're unsure about what constitutes high-quality vs. poor-quality leather and construction, go to an expensive shoe store and try on a few pairs of boots, sandals, or shoes. Notice how the good design actually helps you walk comfortably and smoothly. Remember that even a well-crafted shoe may have a last that is wrong for your foot. Walk around the store and get the feel of different heel heights and styles. Some high heels may throw your balance off, making you feel (and look) uncomfortable. Other shoes and boots with high heels may support you quite well, allowing you to walk with fluidity and speed.

Look for shoes with leather uppers and thin leather insoles. Notice the suppleness and cut of the leather, how it feels on your feet as you walk and turn. If shoes burn your feet, this means that the leather has been improperly tanned. For this reason, and because they do not hold up well, cheaper leather shoes are usually not worth buying. Forget about shoes and boots that are fashioned from man-made materials; they invariably make the feet sweat.

If you haven't realized it already, price should not be your primary concern when you shop for footwear. A well-made pair of expensive pumps that fit you perfectly can last for a decade if you take proper care of them, while a pair of less expensive shoes may deteriorate after only one season of wear. Some high-quality shoe manufacturers that are distributed in the U.K. in department stores and boutiques include Charles Jourdan, Bertie, Sacha, and Ferragamo. All of these designers offer a range of styles from office-conservative to chicly casual to formal dress. Because of the calibre of the materials and the high standards of craftsmanship of any of these shoes, it's worth investing in as

Although high heels are precarious for some women, nevertheless they're an enduring stylish accessory.

Invest in at least one pair of exquisite dress-up shoes. Maintain them lovingly, and you'll delight, disco, and dine in them for years to come.

many pairs as you can afford. After all, shoes reflect your character and are just as important to your image as a subtly tailored skirt or a tastefully styled wristwatch.

SHOE WARDROBE CHECKLIST

To be well-dressed for all occasions, you only need about six pairs of shoes and at least one pair of boots. Here are some specifics:

▶ ONE PAIR of classically cut shoes for your office wardrobe. These should have a medium heel, in anything from a modified wing-tip style that ties to a classic slingback that has a tiny buckle at the side.

▶ TWO MEDIUM-HEEL pumps in suede, leather, or leather and lizard skin. The heels can be narrow or wide, depending on your wardrobe, office environment, and personal taste. Keep in mind that anything wider than two centimeters (three-quarters of an inch) at the top part, where heel and shoe connect, is too chunky and casual looking for your professional image. Get these shoes in basic colours, such as black, brown, or blue.

▶ TWO PAIRS of flats to go with your spring and summer wardrobe.

▶ ONE OPEN-STRAP sandal with a graceful heel that is appropriate for dress and evening wear. Whether the heel is medium or very high, make sure it's delicate enough to look dressy with your special outfits. Black is probably the most versatile colour choice.

▶ ONE PAIR of high-quality leather boots, with heels, in brown or black. (If you can afford it, try to find a pair of dressy boots for more formal winter outfits.)

Naturally, for leisure wear, you should have one pair each of sneakers or running shoes, as well as espadrilles or casual leather sandals, but more about these later.

Styles that Flatter Specific Foot and Leg Shapes

Make your feet appear slimmer and longer with dark-coloured shoes that have seamless vamps. The longer the vamp, the narrower your foot will look. Pointy-toed boots will also add a slimming look. Avoid chunky-heeled footwear.

Downplay thick ankles and/or thick calves by wearing dark-coloured leathers or suedes. Avoid shoes that are shiny or brightly coloured. Never wear boots that are calf height or have flat heels. Get a heeled boot that adds height to your figure and fits slightly loose around the ankles. Shoes and boots with pointy toes will minimize stocky ankles or calves, as will low-vamped shoes. Low-vamped shoes expose a lot of your foot and sometimes the base of your toes. A low vamp gives the illusion of a slimmer lower-leg area and always makes your feet look narrower. Boots that come to mid-calf or two-toned shoes or boots are out of the question for you; they will draw too much attention to your feet and lower legs.

Add more dimension to small-boned ankles and skinny calves with heavy suede shoes and boots, two-toned shoes, and flat boots in leather or suede. You can also try wearing shoes with ornamentation, such as buckles, tassels, and bows. Rounded or squarish toes will also deemphasize skinny calves and ankles.

Large feet will look smaller in low-vamped shoes. To make your feet look shorter and

These flats are made for walking, and you'll really cruise with a matching handbag.

broader, try open-toed shoes. This could mean anything from a pair of dark-coloured pumps with teardrop cutouts in the toe to medium-heeled sandals that expose the entire vamp.

Coordinating Shoes with Any Style Outfit

It's important to develop a sense of what shoes go with which outfits to achieve all kinds of looks—classic, innovative, casual, and elegant. Here are some suggestions for specific styles.

For classic, work-oriented wardrobe looks:

▶ A CLASSIC slingback style with a black patent-leather toe and the rest of the shoe in a cream-coloured leather is a good investment. Sometimes called a "Spectator," this shoe is versatile enough to work with all kinds of dresses and skirts.

▶ BROWN OR black loafers are a conservative, but classic and versatile shoe that can be worn with tweedy skirts, flannel pants, jeans, and linen pants. If penny loafers are too collegiate, try loafers with tassels.

▶ ANY HIGH-HEELED pumps you have—such as those in red or white leather—may be worn with your work wardrobe, of course, but they can also dress up a pair of jeans or casual pants.

▶ FOR A timeless, dressy evening shoe, black satin flats with bows across the vamp are the answer. They're more elegant than patent leather and more versatile, especially if you find a pair that comes with detachable bows that clip on and off. Shoes like these also add a casually chic touch to jeans or cotton pants.

▶ CROCODILE OR two-toned leather and lizard skin medium-heeled shoes make an excellent style and value investment. Reptile skins are extremely durable, adding understated texture and luxury to your work clothes, as well as to casual or semiformal dress or pants ensembles. If you buy a handbag to match your shoes, you'll be classically accessorized for years to come.

▶ CASUAL SHOES such as espadrilles, which are made of canvas and come in flat or heeled styles, are comfortable choices for spring and summer wear. They come in all colours of the spectrum and are moderately priced. One of the drawbacks to espadrilles, however, is that the canvas retains dust and dirt and so becomes discoloured after steady wear. A whisk brush from a hardware store will help dislodge dirt; try to clean your shoes after each wearing, especially if you live in a city or do a lot of walking each day. Another problem with espadrilles is that once the soles, which are usually made of jute with a rubber bottom, wear down, they cannot be replaced. With these classic shoes, however, what you lose in durability you gain in seasonal style, so buying a pair each year may be worth it. Besides, they're great for the beach, and they protect your feet much better than sandals.

Sandals and Summer Shoes

Because summer heat swells feet and causes them to perspire, you should choose sandals on the basis of comfort, material, and support. Generally speaking, however, leather flat-heeled sandals are the best buy. Choose them in a solid colour that coordinates with your warm-weather wardrobe.

BASIC SUMMER STYLES

Here are a few recommendations from the myriad styles you will find:

▶ THONG SANDALS are a simple, comfortable, and classic style, with just one strip of leather between the big toe and its neighbor. This strip of leather is attached to the ankle strap, which usually buckles at the side. An updated version of the thong might replace the buckle with Velcro tab fastenings. As with all sandals, look for a pair that has cushioned innersoles, which will make them more comfortable for miles.

▶ OPEN-TOED ANKLE-STRAP sandals are one of the most popular designs for summer shoes. Accordingly, they come in all heel heights, colours, and materials. Any department store will have a full selection of these, as will most shoe stores.

▶ CANVAS-STRAPPED SANDALS might suit your feet better than leather. Jacques Cohen, maker of espadrilles and other sandals, usually comes up with a palette of beautiful pastels and jewel colours. Look for these in major department stores, finer shoe stores, and resort shops.

▶ HUARACHES ARE South American leather sandals that have been reinterpreted by the shoe industry in all kinds of fashionable styles. There are, for instance, straightforward copies of huaraches that come with medium-stacked heels. There are also many kinds of huarache-derived sandals in a wide spectrum of colours and fine leathers. Because huaraches are woven leather, they are very flexible and allow the feet to breathe.

▶ OTHER CLASSIC sandal designs that look great in casual or dressier versions are Roman sandals, which are open-toed with several decorative straps spanning the foot and ankle; they invariably have flat heels. Fisherman sandals are open-toed, with four crisscrossed straps of leather wrapping around the foot and a side buckle. These sandal styles are also widely available in multicoloured plastic hues, which makes them very good for beach, pool, and summer rainwear.

To save money on your sandals and summer shoes, shop around in dime stores. You can find bargains on all styles, but you must realize that you won't find the most durably made merchandise in these places.

YEAR-ROUND CASUAL STYLES

As previously mentioned, you could use at least two pairs of flats to complement your outfits year-round. These needn't be conventional loafers or slip-ons in boring colours, for flats come in hundreds of variations. Here are some styles that may stimulate your imagination:

▶ SLINGBACKS IN canvas or leather that buckle at the side.

▶ FLATS THAT feature some kind of "decor" across the vamp, such as bows, jewels, silk flowers, or grosgrain ribbon ties.

▶ CANVAS OR leather flats printed with a chintz or paisley pattern.

▶ FLAT LEATHER sandals with long laces that wrap around the ankle and tie at mid-calf.

▶ THIN, REFINED flats cut like men's house slippers, with a graceful, oval toe and low sides.

▶ CANVAS FLATS that are personalized by an embroidered monogram or other decorative design, such as florals, palm trees, or geometrics.

▶ BALLET SLIPPERS in pink, white, black, or gold that can be worn with lightweight dresses, skirts, and pants for semiformal and evening looks. As ballet slippers are rather delicate, don't wear them on the street or to work—save them for dressier occasions.

▶ ALWAYS BEAR in mind that if you find a pair of flats that fit you perfectly but which are available only in boring colours such as white or bone, you can have a shoemaker dye them spring green, fuschia, lavender, royal blue—whatever. Shoe-dyeing doesn't cost much and is undetectable.

A cold-weather wardrobe is ornamentally and functionally enhanced by rugged boots and cozy leggings.

Caring for Leather and Suede

Naturally, the investment you make in your shoes and boots will pay off only if you maintain them well and keep them shined and clean. Here are some cardinal rules:

▶ ALL FOOTWEAR with leather soles—except for evening shoes—must be taken to the shoemaker immediately after purchase for the addition of thin rubber soles. Applying a thin sole layering will make your shoes more likely to last for several years. Additionally, thin rubber taps under the toes of your shoes will prevent them from wearing down; if the heels of your shoes are wide enough, have taps put on there also. Although a maintenance job like this may be expensive, it's worth it in the long run. Be sure to specify the right colour for the additions. A pair of lilac leather pumps, for instance, would look best with a thin black sole that matches its black heels.

▶ IT CANNOT be stressed enough to never let your heels break down so that your shoes look crooked and shabby. At the first sign of overwear, take them to the shoemaker for new heels.

▶ BRUSH SUEDE sandals, shoes, and boots after each wearing with a wire-bristled suede brush. This will keep the finish looking cleaner and brighter. Suede brushes can be purchased at variety stores, shoemakers, and finer shoe stores. Use this brush on your suede handbags and gloves as well.

▶ SHOES AND boots will retain their original shape longer if you insert shoe trees immediately after each wearing. If you don't have shoe trees, stuff your shoes with worn out pantyhose, tissue paper, or newspaper. Or fashion boot trees out of cardboard. Fold or roll the cardboard so that it fits snugly inside the boot and keeps the sides standing up straight. Stuff the toes with tissue paper, newspaper, or old hosiery.

▶ FINE LEATHER shoes and boots deserve to be polished at least once a month to maintain maximum suppleness and shine. There are dozens of shoe polishes on the market, but Meltonian Cream is recommended for fine leathers: it hides scuff marks and shines better than spray-on polish or saddle soap. Wax polish (sold in cans) is recommended for hard-wearing leathers such as winter boots, because it is highly water-resistant. Mink oil is also very good for waterproofing leather shoes and boots, but be advised that it will darken the leather a few shades as it sinks in. Before polishing shoes, brush out any caked mud or grit lying between the sole and the upper with a soft shoe brush. Dust off your shoes with a flannel cloth. Lightly sponge any marks on pastel- or metallic-coloured shoes with a swab of damp cotton or cloth that has been dipped into a bowl of soapy water. Put shoe trees into the shoes and let them dry naturally. When they are dry, work a small amount of cream polish—about the size of a thumbnail—into the shoe with a rag or a soft flannel cloth. Rub the cream in gently with a circular motion. Start at the toe and work around the sides of the shoe, including the heel. Take extra care to apply polish close to where the sole and leather upper meet.

▶ Keeping shoe or boot trees inside as you polish will insure the even distribution of polish, but if you don't have trees, put your hand inside the shoe as far as it will go. After polishing, you can bring up a shine by rubbing the shoe with a genuine chamois cloth, available at shoemakers and finer shoe stores. If you can't find chamois, a chemically treated shoe shine sponge will also do the trick. These also can be bought at shoe stores, shoe makers, or at variety stores.

▶ DON'T WEAR the same pair of shoes two days in a row; they need a day off to air out and dry. Even during winter, shoes and boots absorb a great deal of moisture from your feet. Keep them smelling fresh by wiping the insides with a sponge that has been dipped in a bowl of warm water with a drop or two of ammonia added. You can also sprinkle a small amount of baby powder inside your shoes and boots before and after wearing.

▶ NEVER PLACE shoes or boots near a radiator to dry; this will surely crack the leather or suede. Let them dry naturally in the open air.

▶ CROCODILE AND lizard shoes require minimal care, but they should be carefully dusted with a flannel cloth after each wearing. Never polish lizard shoes; just wipe them with a damp cloth if they're dirty. Crocodile requires an occasional application of neutral shoe cream.

Periodic upkeep measures for leather and suede will add years to your shoes, boots, and sandals.

The smartly accessorized young woman on the right is on firm footing, thanks to her low-heeled leather boots. For a more intriguing bottom half, fishnet stockings and sexy shoes will jazz up any basic black outfit.

Stiletto-heeled shoes are every inch as classic as Coca Cola. What you choose to wear them with is of course dictated by the occasion.

Although buckled flats with dainty straps are not every girl's cup of tea, they are practical and appropriate with classically cut skirts, dresses, or pants.

What to Look for in Boots

Admittedly, as far as accessories go, boots are a high-cost item, but some sage advice comes from fashion and accessories designer Keni Valenti: "If you can't afford to spend a lot of money on clothing or accessories, one way you can upgrade your wardrobe—and your image—is by sinking lots of money into an elegant, expensively crafted pair of boots." The idea is that one great pair of boots will make your outfits look more tailored, more stylish. Also, if you simplify your wardrobe like this, it'll save time on shopping and dressing."

Designers who are known for outstanding boots include: Charles Jourdan, Susan Bennis/Warren Edwards, Gucci, and Peter Fox Shoes. Although all of these have a very costly line, the price is justified by their high quality, durability, and flawless details and craftsmanship. In addition, Peter Fox shoes and ankle high boots come in some of the most unusual colours: mustard, sapphire, ruby red, to name a few.

Major department stores and fashionable boutiques will have a broad selection of designer boots; watch for sales in January or late winter for the best bargains. Hint: Never buy boots with side zippers. The leather inevitably becomes misshapen after prolonged wear, ruining the line of the boot. Additionally, the zippers can catch and snag hosiery, skirts, or pants. If you're cursed (or blessed, in this case) with hard-to-fit feet, you may want to consider a pair of custom-made boots created for you by a shoemaker. Custom boots will probably cost about as much as a designer pair, and imagine how much more comfortable they'll feel on your feet.

Because a well-made pair of leather boots represents a substantial investment, your wisest choice would be a pair of simply styled brown, blue, or black ones that stop just below the knee. The heels should be of medium height, so they will coordinate with the maximum number of skirts, pants, and dresses in your wardrobe. If you live in a cold climate, try to carefully coordinate your boots with your winter coats, hats, scarves, and gloves.

Another classic boot style worth considering is a black, knee-high riding boot. Usually made of durable, thick leather, low-heeled riding boots are extremely comfortable for walking and working. If your wardrobe is rather tweedy or conservative, these boots would make a fitting accessory. Conversely, if you wear mostly monochromatic, dark-coloured, and sharply styled clothes, riding boots would finish your look off with traditional, understated chic. Authentic riding boots can be found at any equestrian shop; imitations are available at most department stores and shoe boutiques.

The boots you buy should be versatile enough to be worn with all the skirts and pants in your closet.

If you like to dress adventurously, you can key entire outfits around a particularly colourful or stylish pair of boots. For example, olive green, calf-high boots would not only match all of the blacks, browns, greens, and blues in your wardrobe, but they'd also go with gray flannel pants or blue jeans. With an olive leather belt or a green scarf, you'd have a distinctively unified outfit. Or use boots in an offbeat colour to contrast with monochromatic clothing. You'll be surprised at the intriguing colour combinations you can come up with if you start experimenting with your basic wardrobe and accessories.

Naturally, long skirts are the best garment with boots of any height. If you have shapely legs, however, try tucking your pants into ankle- or knee-high boots for sporty but chic leisure outfits. And, if you love to dress up in mini skirts, a brightly coloured pair of ankle boots combined with dark pantyhose and a dark skirt is a marvelous combination.

If you're looking for a casual, classic but fun boot, why not consider cowboy boots? In the last twenty years, cowboy boots have evolved from funky footwear to the essence of frontier chic. They come in leather and lizard skin combinations or in plain leathers and basic colours such as bone, burgundy, and black. Some have subtly stitched details, while others are covered with wildly festive, intricate embroidery.

These days, high-fashion shoe designers often do cowboy boot copies in striking colours such as turquoise, pink, or yellow, with coloured leather insets. You can find cowboy boots with low heels, but if you lean towards stylized authenticity, look for stacked heels that cut a clean angle when viewed from the side. Manufacturers such as Tony Lama are known around the world for their high quality and variety of styles; look for cowboy boots in shoe stores, department stores, Western-wear stores, and riding shops.

STYLISH BOOTS FOR DRAMATIC, DRESSY LOOKS

If you like to add extra chic, dash, and line to your outfits, take some time to consider the dozens of options you have in boots—especially when it comes to dressier boots. "Dressy boots" could mean anything from a cherry red leather, pointy-toed style to a pair of black suede knee-highs with wafer thin, flat heels. Think of a pair of dressy boots as the wardrobe accent that will pull your whole look together.

Here are some examples:

▶ WAKE UP a plain black dress or pantsuit with high-heeled, purple suede boots. With a complimentary purple scarf at your neck, you've got a beautifully coordinated outfit.

▶ SPIKE-HEELED, ANKLE-HIGH suede or leather boots are the height of chic when worn with dressy pants and a silk shirt. Black is the most versatile colour. Wear these boots to a disco, a holiday party, or for other special nights on the town.

▶ LOW-HEELED BOOTS made of brocaded tapestry fabric will dramatize monochromatic, heavy- and light-textured skirts and pants alike. Wear them with a sweater that picks up one of the dominant colours in the boot fabric's design.

STORMY WEATHER BOOTS AND OTHER RUGGED STYLES

Depending on your climate, you probably need rainboots or a sturdy pair of outdoorsy boots to wear on muddy spring days. Functional footwear for inclement weather used to mean dreary, black rubber galoshes with jangly buckles. In the last decade or so, however, there's been a trend toward delicately styled, colourful rain boots, and winter styles are more streamlined and attractive, too. Totes is the preeminent manufacturer of rain boots. The company's diverse line ranges from basic black slip-ons that fit over shoes to medium-heeled, pointy-toed waterproof boots that are made from a synthetic fabric that resembles canvas. (These fit directly over the foot and come in mid-calf as well as just-below-the-knee height.) Totes are moderately priced and available worldwide in most department stores, shoe stores, and shoemakers' shops.

Women who enjoy making a fashion statement during a thunderstorm will probably be attracted to the brightly coloured plastic boots made by Fiorucci, the Italian design emporium that has boutiques around the world. Reminiscent of 1960s go-go boots with their pointy toes and spiked heels, these are for the young at heart but short of funds. For not much money, you've got rain or snow boots that look good and fashionable enough to go dancing in!

Because they are made to be sturdy, all-weather boots are not exactly the height of glamour. You can, nevertheless, find plenty of attractive styles in a reasonable price range. The British shoe company Clarks, for instance, makes several tough yet handsome boots. One of their perennially classic styles is a suede desert ankle boot with crepe soles, suitable for casual city or country wear.

Casual boots should be roomy enough to accommodate thick wool winter socks. To get the fit you need, bring different types of socks with you when you are selecting your boots.

On the Top

CHAPTER FIVE:

Historical records show that hats were worn for a multitude of purposes even during the most ancient civilizations. Royal crowns, warrior headdresses, religious habits, and laborers' kerchiefs—these afforded protection and warmth to the wearer, signified social standing, and added dash to men's and women's clothing. People used to cover their heads at all times. Hooded cloaks, head scarfs, and nightcaps were essential garments for rich and poor alike.

One attractive accessory adorns another: a slick pin crowns a wool beret.

Hats Today

Nowadays, thanks to central heating, hats are more of an option than a necessity. If you live in a cold climate, of course, you'll need a warm outdoors hat to protect your head and ears from the elements. But, if you're style-conscious or have a passion for looking ultra-coordinated, hats can be the impressive finishing touch to a total look. The appropriate hat can maximize any outfit by adding stature, importance, and flair to your image.

Once you begin, you'll discover hundreds of ways to use hats to appoint the look or style you are seeking. A hat will draw attention to the jewellery and garments you wear on the upper part of your body. Small pillbox hats or high-crowned fedoras will make short women appear taller. A conservative workday outfit can look many times more stylish with, for instance, a black velvet beret that matches leather shoes, briefcase, and gloves. Hats are especially valuable accessories for evening or formal ensembles; they can add colourful and textural accents that make your look all the more special. Imagine the drama of a broad-brimmed, black felt hat held in place with a faux jewelled hatpin. It would add dash to a classically cut black winter coat or a fake-fur jacket, such as one made of mouton lamb. Or, have you ever considered wearing pillbox hats with veils to give your evening wear a romantic and elegant aura? Whether they're worn for utilitarian purposes or as fashionable decor, hats are a great ally for different seasons and social occasions.

Jane Saks, a millinery designer for Liz Claiborne Accessories, one of North America's leading fashion manufacturers, recommends that you select your hats with regard to these specifics: facial shape, hairline, hairstyle, and, of course, wardrobe. "It's impossible to say which styles look best on a woman, but one rule is that your hat must be in proportion to the size of your head and your particular facial features. Your hats should always be coordinated with an eye towards complementing the colour, style, and texture of your coats and jackets or dresses and sweater, whether you're wearing a cocktail hat or headwrap."

Always carefully match your hat to the garments you're wearing it with, especially if you're going to wear the hat indoors. Jane suggests that you stick to compact, delicate styles such as pillboxes or cloches for hats that are to be worn indoors. Anything too large is bound to appear ostentatious and will block other people's view of the party, restaurant, concert, or whatever. It's also an unwritten fashion rule that hats with veils are to be worn *only* in the late afternoon and evening hours. The exception to this is a veiled hat for a formal occasion such as a wedding or festive afternoon party.

The climate that you live in, as well as your particular sensitivity to cold weather, hot summer sunlight, and precipitation are other factors that will influence your choice of hats. Jane Saks proposes that you consider the following classic hat styles for different seasons and occasions.

Hats for Autumn and Winter

▶ A ONE hundred percent wool beret with casual and work wardrobes. As mentioned previously, the colour of the beret should match your coats and jackets, especially the ones that you wear to work. Berets flatter most face shapes and look dashing in a continental sort of way when worn with sunglasses. Also, berets are relatively inexpensive, so you can afford to have a few in different colours.

▶ A FEDORA, or high-crowned, man-tailored hat in a sturdy felt with a matching grosgrain ribbon band. Darker colours like blue, black, charcoal gray, and brown make the best long-wearing choices, as they will not readily show lint or dirt. Fedoras are more

Fur-trimmed hats keep your head warm and draw attention to sparkling eyes and earrings.

formal-looking and warmer than berets, with good-sized brims that block the wind.

▶ A CLOCHE in felt or one hundred percent wool. The term "cloche" encompasses any close-fitting hat; this can mean a structured felt topper, an angora hat that hugs the head and covers the ears, or a smaller, softer version of a man-tailored hat.

▶ A SCARF hat in sturdy felt, with fabric sewn into the inside of the hat that comes down to cover the ears and tie under the chin. Scarf hats are available in fedora and cloche styles, in dressy and casual versions. A hat like this could be your essential winter headgear; it also lends a very pulled-together look to bulky winter coats.

Hats for spring and summer

▶ A "SILK straw" hat, meaning a thin-strawed hat that is finely and more delicately woven than the typical coarse fibers and chunky weave found in most straw hats and beach bags. Ideally, find a hat in a peri sisal weave, which is characterized by its super-fine and supplely woven texture. Peri sisal is also preferable because the crisp weave will hold its shape no matter how hot the weather. A knowledgeable salesperson should be able to point out the peri sisal hats. If your hat comes with a grosgrain ribbon around the brim, you can dress it up by pinning fresh or silk flowers wherever you like. Or, you can cover the ribbon with a long and narrow silk or cotton gauze scarf. Wrap it around the top of the hat, just above the brim, and tuck the loose ends under the edges of the scarf.

▶ FOR SUNBATHING, you'll need a cap with a long, wide brim. A cotton cap with a

With Paris in the background, any hat is captivating, but a style such as this definitely suits a variety of looks and locales.

duckbill-like brim is an inexpensive and dependable summer hat; so is a white cotton tennis hat, as these usually have tiny air holes at the top of the head. Shop around in sporting goods and variety stores for the best bargains. Another good place to look for low-cost, quality summer caps would be the boys department of a major department store. The lightest and airiest summer caps are given away free at most hardware and paint stores; they're traditional white painter's caps! Although they fall short of high fashion, they're stylish in a funky but chic way when worn with a bathing suit, a casual sundress, or jeans and a T-shirt.

▶ A WATERPROOF rain hat is an optional—although sensible—purchase. Yours can be made of waterproofed canvas, plastic, or thin vinyl. Look for Totes hats in department stores. Or you can make your own rain hat by taking a slightly large tennis hat and spraying it with water-repellent solution.

Dressy looks for autumn and winter

▶ YOU CAN add nighttime dazzle to a beret by pinning on a decorative brooch or pin made of rhinestones, faux pearls, or faux gemstones. Or, if you have a few tiny, delicate pins of different styles, why not fasten these on?

▶ A VELVET beret will dress up a dark-coloured coat and keep you warm in a stylish, classic way.

▶ A CLOCHE or pillbox hat with a veil adds elegance to any semiformal outfit; a veil that comes studded with tiny rhinestones is drop-dead glamourous. If you are skilled with a needle and thread, you could try sewing veils on to hats that you already have. Veils are made of meline netting, available at most fabric shops, sewing supply stores, wholesale/retail millinery companies, and

Top off your evening clothes with a touch of eccentricity. Festooned hats provide delightful counterpoint to real or costume jewels.

sometimes in the sewing sections of major department stores. Attach the netting to the inside of the hat; some people do this with tiny stitches; others suggest using a fast-bonding glue.

▶ FUR-TRIMMED CLOCHES, besides feeling luxurious, are a classic accessory that lend Old World elegance to any tailored winter coat. And, although a fur-trimmed hat is rather costly, it is still a sensible, long-term fashion investment. Sink your money into a well-made, fur-lined hat, if maximum warmth is what you're after in a hat.

Dressy looks for spring and summer

▶ A WHITE peri sisal straw hat with a wide brim and a lacy ribbon or scarf tied round the brim is the perfect "garden party" hat. You might also want to look for a hat that comes with a garland of dried wildflowers around it. Then again, you could weave your own garland out of fresh flowers!

▶ A PASTEL pillbox hat with a matching veil. The hat itself could be made out of brocade fabric, satin or linen.

▶ A PILLBOX or cloche that is festooned with a ribbon bow in the back, or perhaps with feathers. Take into consideration the formality of the occasion, don't spoil your look by wearing millinery that is too ostentatious. You'll make others uncomfortable by your costumed appearance, as well as make yourself unduly self-conscious.

On the Top • 95

When not in use, store hats in the boxes they came in, or protect them with paper bags. Be sure that all hat containers are properly sealed to keep dust, moths, and light away.

Other Headgear

Some women like to supplement their wardrobes with different kinds of shawls, scarves, and cowls. The advantage of accessories like these is that they give a more fluid line to your total look; this can be especially appropriate with voluminous or loose tops, flowing skirts, and full-cut coats. But what are the classic styles, and how can you coordinate, for instance, a paisley print shawl with the clothes that you wear to work? What are the more comfortable fabrics? How should you store silk scarves? Here are some specifics that will help you get maximum wear from these accessories.

HEAD SCARVES

The best size for head scarves is generally a seventy-five centimeter (twenty-seven-inch to thirty-inch) square. This will cover the head adequately with enough material left over for tying neatly and securely under the chin or at the back of the neck.

Without a doubt, silk is the superior fabric for a head scarf because of its warmth, softness, and draping qualities. As opposed to wool, silk is mildew-and moth-resistant, and it's also very slow to wrinkle. It is a rather costly fabric, however, and one of the more fragile ones. You should always have silk scarves—and other silk garments—dry cleaned. Also be advised that silk may yellow or fade from age.

Among the classic patterns for head scarves are paisleys, which coordinate well with tweeds, subtly striped blouses, and knitted wool sweaters. Experiment with patterned clothing and paisleys; most of them can be coordinated in colourful, innovative ways. Geometrics, stripes, abstracts, and flowery chintz-type patterns will also add impact to your coats, jackets, and sweaters.

To store your scarves, fold them neatly into squares and wrap them in white tissue paper. Keep them in a drawer, away from sunlight, for exposure to light can weaken the fabric and make it fade. Chapter Seven, "Wrapping It Up," (See page 112) provides instructions on how to wrap scarves around the head for a variety of classy looks: One bonus to buying head scarves is that their size makes them easy to manipulate into many different styles.

SHAWLS AND HEAD WRAPS

A shawl that works as a shoulder wrap can also be worn around the head, with the remaining fabric wrapped around the neck or tied under the chin. This not only provides a great deal of warmth, but it also looks very dramatic, providing the pattern and fabric weave are of good quality. A fine cashmere and silk blend is best for this type of garment, as it is very soft and warm, yet lightweight. An accessory like this can be expensive, but it would be a warm and fashionable ally to your winter wardrobe. Department stores usually have the greatest selection of shawls and head wraps; it's conceivable that you could get a very good price on one during a sale. Ask a salesperson when the next sale is planned.

COWLS

For ultra-warm and stylish headgear, nothing matches a wool cowl that fits over the head. A tube-shaped piece of wool, it covers you from the top of your head, over your ears, and stops at the base of the neck. If you know how to knit, you can fashion your own in a few hours. All you have to do is knit an oblong that is wide enough to cover your head and neck. Check to see if your piece is large enough, then stitch it up with matching thread. Or, if you want a more colourful or textural finish to the cowl, use a metallic or bright-coloured thread like turquoise or red that will make an interesting seam. Angora wool is a good choice for this project, as it is softer and less likely to irritate your skin than other wools.

KNIT CAPS AND HATS

As soon as autumn rolls around, a myriad of casual and semidressy wool hats and caps are available in stores everywhere. These come in handy for winter sports and general cold-weather wear. In sporting goods stores and ski shops—or in boutiques or department stores that offer more stylish millinery—you can find dozens of different looks. A tightly knit, imported ski cap, however, could cost you a bit of money, though you would be getting a lifelong accessory for your money. But, if you're interested in more moderately priced winter hats and caps, ones made of acrylic or a wool and acrylic blend will cost less than those of one hundred percent wool. Other relatively inexpensive, quality hats and caps are Irish and Scottish wool knits. The wools from Iceland are also very warm and comfortable.

SPECIAL HEADGEAR FOR FESTIVE OCCASIONS

Accessorizing dress-up clothes with a decoratively tied head scarf, head wrap or bow can lend unmistakable flair to your apparel. Here are some specifics:

▶ WRAP A lustrous scarf around your head like an Indian turban.

On the Top • 99

If the weather is extreme, you're in between shampoos, or you want a change, take a tip from the headgear styles pictured. You can turn any hairstyle or weather disadvantages into fresh, fashionable accessory opportunities.

▶ IF YOU have a well-proportioned face and/or a high hairline, show off these features to their best advantage with a black velvet head wrap that matches your semiformal or formal black garments. To achieve a really special look, style your hair accordingly. If your hair is long, curl it so that it tumbles back from the head wrap in a soft halo. Conversely, if your hair is short or medium-length, slick it back with gel or, if you have bangs, fringe some wisps of hair over the front of the head wrap.

▶ FOR HOLIDAY parties, formal dances, or any stylish event, a glamourous accessory that can give your ensemble a coordinated dazzle is a big, beautiful bow tied around your head. Consider the possibilities: black velvet for classic chic, a thick length of black or cream lace, for a softer look or shiny black, gold, or silver taffeta for more drama. A decorative wrapped bow is one way of adding colour to your appearance without having to rely on makeup, which invariably fades over the course of an evening. Additionally, the bow can mesh or contrast with the colours and texture of your clothing, making it a very useful accessory. You could easily make your own bow by purchasing a special fabric and sewing it up neatly. Sew on sequins or pearl beads, glue on some white rhinestones, or attach some pretty lace to the ends.

Singin' in the Rain

Ever since nylon, retractable umbrellas were invented, the awkwardness of carrying an umbrella has lessened. For those whose tastes rule out retractables, however, there are still many full-length styles from which to choose. One rule to remember: Coordinate your umbrella not only with your raincoat, but with your briefcase, shoulder bag, and rainboots as well. Granted, for some women, an ultra-coordinated rainy ensemble is hardly essential: Most people don't care what they look like in stormy weather! But if you happen to be dressing for success, realize that your raingear is just as much a part of your image as your winter coat, boots, and hats. Also, on dreary damp days, it can be a great spirit-lifter if you dress in a well-coordinated or colourful way, instead of trudging along with a drab umbrella that you bought in a hurry one drizzly afternoon.

RETRACTABLE UMBRELLAS

Because they're lightweight and compact, retractables are easy to fit into a shoulder bag or briefcase. You can also find them at rock-bottom prices in variety stores, at shoemaker shops, and on the street. Be aware, though, that unless you get a good-quality, brand-name model, such as one by Totes or London Fog, a low-cost umbrella is often a victim of planned obsolescence and will fall apart after only a few months of rainy days. As far as special features go, more expensive umbrellas, such as London Fogs, have sturdy, thick handles with molded finger grips, which make them more comfortable to carry.

Tote along an umbrella built for two to protect you and a friend on romantic, rain-soaked walks.

And when the skies have cleared, you can tote the umbrella around your wrist, thanks to the attached vinyl handle strap.

Designer umbrellas

Designer umbrellas are uniformly of good quality, although designs consisting of bold initials or prominent signatures can lend an overly promotional aspect to your appearance. If you want to keep your image classic and uncluttered, steer clear of these types. In most cases, anyway, "designer" umbrellas are not actually created by top couturiers such as Bill Blass, Calvin Klein, or Hubert de Givenchy. Many designers simply sell their names under licensing agreements to particular manufacturers, so if you think you're paying for a fashion leader's personal design, you may be wrong! As when purchasing any accessory, however, the prime imperative is to select one that works with everything you have. If there is a designer umbrella that particularly suits you, then of course, go ahead and buy it.

Classic umbrellas and style suggestions

If your taste runs towards the traditional, and you can afford to spend a little more, one classic-style umbrella would be a canvas, nonretractable model with a polished wooden handle. Department stores invariably carry a selection of these in a dozen or so colours; a classic hue, such as gray, black, navy blue, or red will not readily show stains or dirt. If you really want to go all out, look for an umbrella with a decorative handle. Duck's heads and faux knotty wood are perennially chic, in a country gentry way. Hint: Read the label first to confirm that the fabric is waterproof.

For added convenience, you might want to get a full-sized umbrella that comes with a detachable canvas shoulder strap. When it's not raining, you can close the umbrella and walk freely with it slung over your shoulder. On the days when you do feel like carrying it in your hand, all you have to do is unhook the strap from the handle and go.

A high quality umbrella is a rainy day friend.

Umbrellas for colour lovers

▶ CHINESE AND Japanese parasols are perhaps the most colourful and artistically designed rainwear. With straight wooden handles and varnished paper umbrellas painted with flowering vines, mountain scenery, and the occasional kimonoed geisha, they are inexpensive, very utilitarian, and distinctive. Although they'd look a trifle out of whack with a classic trench coat, they are perfect for the more casual, stylized, or nonconformist dresser during spring and summer showers. Look for Oriental parasols in import shops, at flea markets, and in Chinese neighborhoods.

▶ NOW THAT flowery chintz patterns are all the rage, a pastel print might be just the thing for a warm-weather umbrella.

▶ TRANSPARENT VINYL umbrellas are a slick alternative to somber, dark colours. Their see-through fabric also allows for better visibility for walking at nighttime.

▶ YOU CAN design your own umbrella by colouring a beige or pastel one with permanent ink, which is waterproof. You can draw seascapes, rainscapes, polka dots and stripes, your *own* initials, or geometrics.

Umbrellas for two

For people who like to walk in the rain together, there happen to be umbrellas that are made to accommodate two people. These can be especially useful, however, for the single woman who by necessity has to carry home her groceries, handbag, briefcase, and a variety of other belongings at the end of a damp day. An oversized umbrella will keep leather goods and parcels warm and dry, not to mention yourself! Look for these at major department stores, accessory boutiques, and specialty shops. Although they're more expensive than most umbrellas, the added convenience they provide justifies the expense.

SATCHEL STYLE

Chapter Six:

Purses, handbags, clutches or pouches—women carry various models of these wherever they go, day or night. Because a handbag contains the essential tools and accoutrements of leisure and professional life, it's an indispensable accessory—like a wristwatch—and its form *must* follow function. In the final analysis, a handbag is as much an accessory to your wardrobe as it is to *yourself,* since it is on your person, by your side, for hours every day.

Conventional fashion wisdom used to dictate that a bag *had* to be the same colour as a woman's shoes, or she risked appearing improperly dressed for social occasions and office work. Ever since the revolution in style and colour that characterized the 1960s and 1970s fashion scene, however, rules like these have relaxed to the point of blurring altogether. Especially in leisure wear, your handbag can be whatever colour or texture you want it to be. If you're in the business world, naturally, certain unspoken rules prevail: Because it's so visible, one's handbag must be in keeping with the image one wants to project. Whether your bag is of fine Florentine leather or of textured vinyl, it must be in perfect repair at all times. This means no stains, scuff marks or unraveling straps; no worn edges, damaged zippers or clasps.

Generally speaking, you should keep your handbags in the same colour scheme as your wardrobe. For example, if you wear mostly dark colours, a classic, unadorned, black leather shoulder bag should carry you through in style. If funds permit, you can invest in colourful bags that will accent your clothing, shoes, hats, and scarves. Women who like to be ultra-coordinated at all times can buy handbags, shoes, and belts that match each other and pull any look together—the finishing touch of smart chic.

Bags for Work and Casual Wardrobes

With literally thousands of designs to choose from in myriad colours, materials, and shapes, perhaps the best way to decide on the right shoulder bag for your needs is by the process of elimination. For instance, if your wardrobe is very tailored and "dress for success" oriented, you can rule out most casual designs and materials such as oversized leather pouches, tapestry bags, shoulder bags with trendy colours, hardware, or detailing, or those made of canvas, vinyl, or nylon. The styles that will enhance your professional image are subdued, traditional, and made of high-quality leather (or vinyl that can pass for leather), with unobtrusive stitching and detailing. Additionally, the buckles or grommet closures must be of sturdy gold- or silver-tone metal that will stand up to long wear. If they're made of brass, it will be necessary to polish them often.

Needless to say, any handbag that you carry every day must be sturdily constructed or it simply won't hold up as long as it should. For women who dislike shoulder bags and need some tasteful alternatives, there are certain styles, such as two-handled purses and totes, that are more practical for your needs. The handles should be wide enough to fit over your wrist; smooth leather ones would be the most comfortable and durable. You can find purses like these in any department store or women's shop in such materials as leather, canvas, and vinyl. Be advised that leather is the longest-wearing material, as well as the most stylish.

Naturally, if you carry a briefcase with you to work, a neatly proportioned shoulder bag is the most practical choice for you. On the other hand, if all you need is a good quality, well-designed durable bag, you might be interested in a two-handled purse, a pouchy canvas or vinyl shoulder bag, or a lightweight nylon tote.

Department stores, such as Miss Selfridge's in Britain or Macy's in the U.S., have a varied collection of moderately priced leather and vinyl purses; their styles are very popular with working women because they are also chic in an understated way. More expensive designers, such as Louis Vuitton and Gucci, have several variations on two-handled purses. Although both of these lines feature bags bedecked with designer initials, they have nevertheless achieved a certain classic fashion status around the world, due in part to their elite cachet but primarily to their fine, durable workmanship. Look for these bags at major department stores and upscale boutiques.

OTHER SHOULDER BAGS

Many women will find shoulder bags particularly appropriate with their work wardrobes. The most attractive and functional style is a rectangular shoulder bag with slim straps, which comes in both large and small sizes. Look for a bag made of thick but pliable leather with a grommet closure on the fold-over flap in front and a zippered inside pocket. If properly cared for, a well-made shoulder bag should hold up for a decade or more. You can condition it with mink oil (which will darken the leather slightly) and clean it with saddle soap and water. Use a cotton cloth for both procedures.

For a real standout bag, look for a pebble-textured leather streamlined saddlebag with real brass fittings. It will probably represent a major investment, but a bag as durable and handsome as this is of unquestionably superior value. It will come in several colours, but black, burgundy, or taupe are probably the best choices for a professional wardrobe.

More casual leather shoulder bag styles would include the widely imitated "hobo" bag, originated by Tony Bryant Designs of New York. This is a simple, pouchy bag whose top half folds over in a neat flap. Another popular style is a pouch that closes at the top by matching leather drawstring pulls. Look for a pouch, whether medium-sized or oversized, that is made of durable leather with long, adjustable straps. A long strap can be draped over your head and across your shoulder, so that the bag hangs securely comfortably at your side, slightly behind you. Wearing the bag this way will also free both of your arms, which is especially useful if you do a lot of walking.

If you prefer super-sleek, compact shoulder bags, you'll find a plethora of styles both up-to-the-minute and very affordable. A visit to any major department store's handbag counter will offer dozens of designs suitable for daytime and nighttime occasions.

Canvas shoulder bags

Although they lack the polish and allure of leather goods, canvas shoulder bags are nevertheless quite fashionable and are considerably less expensive. Canvas bags work with casual and summer work wardrobes and are easily matched with canvas belts, espadrilles, and large tote bags. Because canvas takes colour well, you can find bags in dozens of classic and more unusual hues, as well as artfully silk-screened bags with figurative and abstract patterns. Here are some canvas styles to look for:

▶ SADDLEBAGS IN compact, medium, and large sizes with three compartments, one of which is a zippered, inside pouch that is useful for personal items. The bags are often trimmed in leather, with leather straps and delicate-looking but sturdy buckles. They come in about a dozen different colours.

▶ UPDATED HUNTING bags with outside compartments that close by a leather strap and buckle. These come in many colours and are great for the beach, the office, or visits to the library.

▶ ROOMY, SQUARISH bags with front flaps that buckle closed over outside compartments. You'll find these in large and small sizes in a rainbow of colours from dove gray to olive green to violet. The straps are usually leather, and the bags have inside compartments as well.

Caring for Canvas

To insure a long life for your canvas bag, Russell Bryant of Tony Bryant Designs suggests that you regularly brush it clean with a straw-bristled whisk brush, sold in hardware stores and supermarkets. "A few quick flicks of the brush will keep the bag's colour looking brighter longer," Bryant says. "Brush it once a week and you may add a few years to the bag."

Do a little research to zero in on the right casual shoulder bag for you. Don't settle for the first bag that catches your fancy, but comparison shop at boutiques, department stores, and leather goods shops.

A soft shoulder bag is a key feature of casual sportswear ensembles.

SOFT SHOULDER BAGS

Those of you who prize lightweight, easy portability in a shoulder bag will want to consider the many styles available in "soft shoulder bags"—bags fashioned from natural and man-made materials that can stylishly accommodate your personal belongings without weighing you down. The trendsetting handbag and luggage line, Le Sportsac, features dozens of comparatively featherweight shoulder bags made of long-wearing, rip-stop nylon that easily expands to carry lots of cargo, if need be. Notable for their clean, high-tech designs, Le Sportsacs feature many models that have outside zippered compartments. Every handbag or shoulder bag comes folded up in a matching zippered pouch that allows you to store the bag when its not in use. This pouch also makes an excellent cosmetic bag, document pouch, or jewellery case. Le Sportsac has a line of handbags and luggage called Elements, made of lightweight canvas in a variety of small to roomy to oversized designs. Look for Le Sportsac bags in department stores and luggage stores; they are available almost everywhere and often come in fun patterns and colours.

Especially for warm-weather wardrobes, a colourful cotton shoulder bag, such as one with a flowery chintz print, bold stripes, or geometrics, can be a perfect accompaniment to relaxed, casual clothing. Loose-fitting garments such as tunics, oversized T-shirts, gauzy skirts, and pyjama-cut pants are best balanced by a shoulder bag that echoes the shape and line of free-flowing clothing styles. Some possible choices in cotton shoulder bags might include:

▶ A PATTERNED oval pouch with a shoulder strap that is the same material as the bag can be an accent to pastel clothes or summer whites. Tropical prints or polka dots are pretty patterns for summer.

▶ A COTTON "tapestry" bag will coordinate with practically all of your garments. The woven design also will add texture and dimension to your total look.

▶ AN ALL black cotton bag might be the best investment you can make, as it will not show dirt and can double as a "dressy" summer bag. A bag with lots of compartments might even work as a weekend bag.

A WORD ABOUT VINYL BAGS

Manufacturers and designers have been experimenting with synthetic materials like vinyl and have refined the production to the point where, today, vinyl goods are a casually fashionable alternative to natural leather accessories.

As a shoulder bag material, vinyl's advantages are distinctly practical. For starters, vinyl is cleaned easily and almost impossible to stain; unless you spill ink or nail polish on it, vinyl will wipe clean without any traces. A textured vinyl bag, whether it's ribbed or pebbly, also will stand up to repeated wear and not scratch as easily as finer leathers. Last but not least, vinyl is usually markedly less expensive than leather. So, be sure you don't rule out vinyl bags—or belts, for that matter—before carefully considering the pros and cons.

Some of the most attractive and popular textures in vinyl bags are vertical, "tire look" stripes; raised polka dots and crosses; simulated crocodile and water buffalo hides. Any of these styles would complement the textures of leather or suede shoes, jackets, belts, and gloves.

OVERSIZED SHOULDER BAGS AND TOTES

Some of the most deservedly popular oversized shoulder bags are available at department stores like Harrod's. Their canvas hunting bag has a roomy interior, an adjustable canvas strap, and leather trim. Available in colours like navy, green, and natural cream/white, this bag is a great value.

Since the resurgence of ethnic handcrafts a few years ago, woven straw Kenyan shoulder bags in earth-tone colours have become a cult fashion classic. With high-quality leather straps and closures, these bags are rather heavy when empty, but they nevertheless hold a lot of items and protect them well. Whether you use yours as a beach bag or a summer carryall, the larger sized ones are inexpensive, durable totes.

The Danish Schoolbag is *the* prototype for many of today's oversized shoulder bags. It is a large, squarish bag with an outside flap that folds over to buckle closed with canvas straps. There's a zippered compartment on the outside flap and an outside pocket on the back of the bag that is perfect for newspapers and magazines. There are two snap-closure pockets under the front flap of the bag and compartments for pencils and documents. Identification labels are attached to the inside as well. The wide canvas strap is adjustable. The bag just described, which comes in a dozen or so colours, is the basic model; there are larger sizes with more compartments that are more expensive.

Two-handled boat and tote bags are available at nautical supply stores, marinas, and camping stores. Used by boaters and workmen for many years, these canvas bags will carry everything from ice blocks to beach gear, library books, or groceries. Look for a

A well-made, sturdy, oversized tote bag may be all the luggage you'll ever need.

The pouch bag above is a perennially popular, international style. Liz Claiborne's classic and coordinated handbags, belts, hats, and shawls are recommended for young, professional, no-nonsense wardrobes.

bag like this in white heavy cotton duck. You'll probably find bags made of the heaviest materials at a nautical supply store.

For carrying around town, any solid-coloured or print canvas tote will be suitable for your day-to-day needs. Totes with leather handles are recommended for their long wear. If you desire something tote-ish that has more flair than the average style, check out the designer handbags section of any major department store. You should find something that satisfies both your sense of aesthetics *and* your practical needs.

Leather tote bags, of course, are the first and last word in spacious, classic hand luggage. You'll find them in many different colours and models. Some have zippers, compartments, and grand dimensions; some are as simply designed as the aforementioned boat and tote bag. A worthwhile leather tote bag, however, will be expensive. Buying one in a darker colour will insure that you can use it for many a season, though.

Another leather tote worth considering is an all-leather backpack, a more urbane version of the classic camping bag. These, too, are on the costly side, but they're very convenient for carrying around town and they leave your arms free for holding packages, bicycling, or whatever.

Briefcases

Now that women comprise a significant portion of the work force, briefcases are not only in, they're an absolute necessity. Like it or not, if you want to be a success in your profession, you must dress like one. Your briefcase is a prime example; even if you're an administrative assistant, it must be of a design and material eminently suitable for a meeting with the chairman of the board. It should also be of fine-quality leather that matches your purse or shoulder bag. Here are some briefcase do's and don'ts:

BRIEFCASE DO's

▶ DO INVEST in a water buffalo briefcase. The water buffalo leather is beautifully textured and more durable than fine leather. Most important, an accessory like this will last a good decade or more before it shows signs of wear. Get one with an overall design that is slender and free of ornamentation, with several accordionlike compartments on the inside. Black is the most versatile colour, and it will, of course, need less care than a tan briefcase.

▶ DO LOOK for an envelope—a leather case without straps or handles—if fine, smooth, glossy leather is your preference. The interior should have compartments for your different papers and other business articles.

▶ DO FIND a briefcase that has retractable handles that slide down and disappear into the sides, if you like a clean line in a briefcase but find envelope styles unsatisfactory for your needs. You can carry the case as an envelope when you wish and pull out the handles when you've got several other things to carry home with you. The handles, of course, should be of matching leather.

▶ DO WATERPROOF your briefcase with spray-on water-repellent or mink oil if you want to get maximum use out of your investment. Most luggage stores sell these formulas on the premises; ask a salesperson which kind is best-suited for the briefcase of your choice.

BRIEFCASE DON'Ts

▶ DON'T BUY a briefcase that comes emblazoned with designer's initials. Although initialed bags are fine for carrying over your shoulder, they're distracting and unprofessional for carrying to meetings, interviews, and conferences.

▶ DON'T BUY a briefcase with an attached shoulder strap if you're striving for an ultraclassic professional image. A shoulder strap makes the briefcase look like a casual and somewhat awkward appendage to your work wardrobe.

▶ DON'T USE a briefcase that is on the bulky or wide side. These may be typical styles for men, but large dimensions are less than flattering to a professional business woman's total look.

▶ DON'T SELECT a briefcase that sports combination locks and excess hardware unless you definitely need features like these for carrying precious documents and artic-

A briefcase can unify your wardrobe by helping you do business with professional flair and efficiency.

All dressed up and no place to go? Sling the right bag over your shoulder and you'll be ready for whatever the night brings.

les. Most businessmen and women who travel always have their briefcases by their sides. If you're afraid of checking your case at a restaurant, then bring it to the table with you.

▶ DON'T GET your initials monogrammed on the briefcase unless you can afford to get a very good job done. Stay away from do-it-yourself monogrammed initials; instead, have the process done at the store where you buy the briefcase.

Evening Bags, Dress Purses, and Clutches

The type of social life you lead will generally determine what kinds of dressier bags are appropriate for your dates and special occasions. If you'd like to have one classic dress bag that's suitable for every occasion, though, you'll find it in a black velvet clutch with a decorative clasp closure. If you prefer leather to match your gloves and shoes, however, look for a sleek leather clutch that closes with a dressy clasp. Evening bags with zippers just aren't quite as glamourous as those with clasps. Faux-jewelled clasps or gilded ones add ornamentation that highlight your earrings and other jewellery, as well as dress up a basic black dress or jacket-and-pants ensemble.

Take the lead from the type of outfits that you wear and the accessories that you favor: If you wear a lot of classic outfits with pearls, for instance, silver- and gold-mesh bags would be right in keeping with your ensemble. If you like to wear a lot of sparkling jewellery like rhinestones, gemstones or crystals, beaded clutches or bags with delicate metallic straps are the thing for you.

If you have a primarily solid-coloured wardrobe, inject your clothing with pop culture overtones, courtesy of vintage psychedelic accessories or '80s updates of the same.

Perhaps the most decorative and refined of evening bags is the *minaudière*, a small case made of a hard material such as sterling silver, tortoiseshell trimmed in eighteen-karat gold, or mother-of-pearl encrusted with faux gemstones. Most *minaudières* are meant for carrying in the hand, although several styles come with silk cords, gold-tone chains, or faux pearled strands for wearing over the shoulder. You can find *minaudières* in most major department stores. If you need and can afford one in a high-price range, by all means, take it home with you; it's a *de luxe* accessory for formal dinner parties, formal weddings, the opera, or the ballet.

Less formal evening bags could include anything from lizard-skin or crocodile clutches to skinny shoulder bags in the same materials. Satin purses are also a perennial choice for tasteful evening bags; other materials that might suit you are patent leather—in black, of course—and heavy brocaded silk. The main quality you should look for in an evening bag is delicacy. So choose a bag that's small and subtly designed, but one that adds dressy zing and flair to your clothing and jewellery. And don't forget: It must coordinate with your evening shoes, either as an accent or as a similarly coloured and similarly designed accompaniment.

Small Leather Goods

For those who have a passion for perfectly coordinated purse-accessories, small leather goods such as credit- and business-card cases, key cases, coin purses, and lipstick cases are the final touches to a pulled-together look. Look for these at major department stores or accessory boutiques.

WRAPPING IT UP

Chapter Seven:

Key accessories like belts, scarves, and gloves can add much more than a dash of colour or texture to your wardrobe. What makes them special—in an overall, fashion-enhancing sense—is that you can mix a belt, scarf, or gloves with an outfit and create a more unified, stylish look that is absolutely your own. A case in point: You have a gray wool blazer and skirt suit that is a mainstay of your work wardrobe. Although this suit is a classic, no matter how you accessorize it—with pearl earrings, textured hose, whatever—you feel more schoolmarmish than businesslike and as if you look like the majority of women on the streets. If you add a simple, ornamental flourish, however, like a burgundy silk pocket scarf, you could dandify and individualize this suit, and elevate it to ensemble status.

At the other end of the fashion spectrum, casual clothes like T-shirt dresses, tunics, and jumpsuits can be stylized and improved by teaming them with all kinds of belts, woven waist wraps, or scarves. The basic idea is to integrate your disparately designed garments with the line, proportion, and detail of carefully chosen accessories.

Continuing in this imaginative vein, the right pair of gloves can reinforce your total look and/or accent the balance of your handbag, shoes, jewellery, and belt. Gloves are an excellent accessory to use for special colour effects. Add a pair of raspberry coloured leather gloves, for example, to revive your winter coat and hat ensemble. And for evening or other special occasions, who can deny the allure of buttery soft, black suede, elbow-length gloves?

Whether you're interested in developing maximum style options, in giving your basics a new, fresh look, or you just want to get a better idea of which fashions are right for your figure and lifestyle, experimenting with belts, scarves, and gloves is one of the easiest ways to refine and redesign your individual, basic wardrobe. Let your common sense guide you, but also rely on your instincts. Don't hesitate to try what at first seem like outrageous coordinations—an unusual colour combination or an unexpected texture. You'll be sure to come up with some appealing surprises.

Sash yourself in belts of striking textures, eyecatching colours, and dramatic widths. For very little cost, you can buy a few belts—or make your own—so you can modify and enhance the look of your dresses and separates.

Belts

To begin, your choice of belts is obviously related to the particular tailoring of your wardrobe. Whether your closet is dominated by crisply classic clothes, body-hugging separates, or loosely cut, romantic fashions, there are several specific belt styles that you'll want to consider because they'll make your clothes more versatile. And, if you're especially fond of the layered look, belts are a major ally in holding it all together. To give you some preliminary ideas, here are suggestions for a few versatile belt styles that you should be sure to have on hand to spice up your work, casual, and evening wardrobes.

Work wardrobe belts

▶ ONE SMALL buckled belt in leather or snakeskin, in a colour that matches your winter suits and skirts. The most versatile width is probably two and a half centimeters (one inch), but this will depend on your garments. Whether the buckle is gold- or silver-tone is a matter of personal taste; naturally, if you wear mostly gold jewellery, you'll want the buckle to match.

▶ ONE SIMPLY styled leather belt to wear with tailored, between-season outfits, such as lightweight suits or dresses, or linen skirt-and-blazer combinations.

▶ AT LEAST three differently styled belts to wear with jackets, blouses, pants, and loose-fitting dresses. If you favor long sweaters over pants and skirts in the winter, you might want to belt these. For shirts with

pants, a wide pull-through adjustable belt with a large buckle is a versatile choice; get it in basic black leather. For warm-weather dresses and tunics, a wide reversible wrap, is the perfect solution. For winter wool and other heavy-fabric dresses, why not try a wide, constructed belt that is reinforced with a lining, to give it a fuller, more appropriate shape for complementing knits and tweeds? This belt could be a thick leather or suede wrap that ties at the side or in front.

Casual wardrobe belts

▶ A LEATHER, Western-style belt to wear with jeans, big shirts, and with casual skirts also works nicely with saddlebags and most other leather shoulder bags. If you own a pair of cowboy boots, then a Western belt is practically a necessity.

▶ ONE BRASS-BUCKLED, narrow canvas belt in a bright or pastel colour that matches your summer shoes and handbags.

▶ LONG SCARVES can double as waist wraps for shirting dresses or tunics, so try experimenting with them.

Dressy and evening belts

Because dressing up means different things to different women, you may find that some of the following belt styles would enhance your daytime wardrobe as well. So much the better. Occasional day-for-night dressing can add a touch of chic when you need it, besides saving you the trouble of adding or subtracting accessories before you go out in the evening. Still, remember to exercise caution when choosing a snazzy belt for work. If you think it might be just a tad too conspicuous for the typical style of your office, tuck it into your purse for after hours!

▶ VERSATILE, GLAMOUROUS, and comfortable, a very wide leather or suede waist

Studded belts never go out of style. They're ideal for coordinating with jumpsuits and if the mood strikes you, they'll imbue your image with a flash of biker chic.

wrap could be one of your most valuable accessories. Add a smartly cut wrap to classic black pants and a crisp white shirt, for example, and turn your outfit into a tuxedolike ensemble that is perfect for any semiformal occasion. If your wrap has a decorative buckle, this detail will make it unique, more versatile, and easier to accessorize. Wear your wrap with a basic black dress, a sweater dress, or even, if you like, with a tunic and jeans.

▶ PATENT LEATHER has long been one of the most fashionable materials for semiformal and formal shoes and handbags. A glossy patent-leather belt, however, can be worn with a dozen different outfits to achieve similarly swank effects. Whether your belt is wide or narrow; gold, or patent leather buckled, see how well it will mix with the different fabrics in your wardrobe. For instance, linen, cashmere, and wool jersey all look surprisingly good with patent leather. If you have a trim waistline, a patent-leather belt is one of the most becoming ways to accentuate it.

▶ A SNAKESKIN belt is another high-fashion accessory that adds polish to daytime or nighttime jacket-and-skirt or pants ensembles. You might want to get one in a classic, dark tone, but then again, if you like your belts to *accent* your garments, colours like deep red, electric blue, or green might be more useful. Naturally, a jewelled belt buckle will add even more shine and flash to your ensembles.

▶ STUDDED BELTS come in simple and ornate styles; let your taste determine what looks fitting with the design and general spirit of your separates. A black leather belt with geometric studs (squares, triangles, or circles) can be worn with daytime or evening pants, over tunics and sweaters, or with dresses and skirts of various fabrics and designs. A faux gem-studded belt will add fi-

Take but a few seconds to pull together your outfit with an artfully tied fabric sash.

nal touch sparkle to jeans, dressier skirts, dresses, or pantsuits.

▶ IF YOU want to invest in an unusual, all-purpose belt, why not get a leather one with a sterling silver buckle? Although it might cost you a lot, you'll recoup your investment by wearing it for the rest of your life. (In general, this kind of shopping will save you money.) A silver-buckled belt in a subtle style can be worn to the office, out to dinner, with leisure wear, or to a discotheque. Just be sure to polish the buckle every so often and replace the belt part when the leather starts to look worn.

▶ DARK-COLOURED VELVET, satin, or metal-chain mesh belts are all likely candidates for dressier daytime ensembles. And of course, they're eminently suitable for pairing with evening wear. A belt in any one of these materials can be readily coordinated with the majority of formal-style clothes and fabrics. Additionally, these sorts of belts are easily accessorized with classic jewellery like pearls, crystals, silver, and gold. When it comes to matching your shoes to one of these belts, also think classic: Basic black leather pumps or flats can just as easily complement a gold-tone mesh belt as they can a gray satin or black velvet belt.

Cheap Chic Belt Bargains

If a limited clothing budget prevents you from collecting as many belts as you'd like, here are some tips on how to get more belts for your money:

▶ IF YOU have a small waist, shop around in the boys' and girls' departments of large retail stores.

▶ IF YOU like studded belts and have an artistic bent, you can make your own for next to nothing. Jewellery and trimming-supply stores usually sell dozens of different kinds of studs, from pearl to metal to faux gems. With an assortment of these and a stud gun, you have the tools to decorate a plain leather belt. You can also stud your own gloves and scarves or even your leather or denim jackets, your jeans, or your hats.

▶ BEADED LEATHER belts are the kind of novelty accessory that look great with jeans, casual pants, and skirts. The intricate, American Indian-inspired beading is a natural accessory to Western clothing. Buy these belts in souvenir shops, and for the price, you'll have a fun conversation piece.

▶ IF YOU find a high-quality canvas or leather belt on sale, but it's too large, remember that you can still make it fit; take it to a shoe- or leather-repair shop and have a hole punched just where you need it. The extra length of leather can be tucked in behind the buckle for a stylish, menswear flourish.

▶ ESPECIALLY LONG faux pearl necklaces or metal chains dangling with whimsical charms can be worn through the belt loops of your jeans and other leisure pants to make a chic, ornamental belt.

Belt advice

Depending on your body type, the belt you wear can emphasize or camouflage a figure flaw. The following guidelines should help you zero in on the belts that will be most flattering to your shape:

▶ IF YOU want to minimize a heavy middle, avoid wide belts, waist sashes, and any tight-fitting belts. Instead, use a narrow belt of the same fabric or colour as the dress, pants, or skirt you are wearing. Avoid belts of bright material, like patent leather or eyecatching colours. Also steer clear of gold-mesh belts and pastel leathers.

▶ IF YOU want to add height to your silhouette, concentrate on finding belts in colours that are perfectly matched to your clothing. This will keep the visual line unbroken from top to bottom. If you want the effect all the way, belts of the same fabric as your dresses or skirts will be ideal for your aim.

▶ IF YOU are high waisted, a belt slung around your hips will divert attention from this characteristic. A thin belt that wraps loosely twice also would be a good choice for your body type.

▶ IF YOU want to appear shorter, break the line of your dresses and separates with belts in contrasting colours. Big-buckled belts would be fine for your body type: so would waist wraps and sashes.

▶ IF YOUR build is very slender, wear wide belts, waist wraps or scarves to even out your lower body's proportions and create the appearance of a fuller figure.

How to tie waist wraps and sashes

A loose-cut dress becomes more stylized with a wide scarf or sash double-wrapped at the waist. When choosing a waist wrap, be sure that the fabric is of a weight and texture that harmonizes with the dress or skirt material. If you're dressing for night, you might want to wear an extra-long wrap woven with glittery, metallic threads. To tie a waist wrap, place it at the front of your waist. Wrap the ends to the back, cross them, and bring them back to the front. Tie at the side in a big bow or tuck in the ends of the scarf for a more finished effect.

For sleekly fitting knit dresses, skirts, and pants, wrap a sash low at the hips. To tie, place the sash at the hips in back. Bring the ends around in front, cross them, twist, then tuck them under the already wrapped edge of the scarf.

Another way to style sashes at the waist or hip is to pin the sash in place with a large brooch, or use a few special rhinestone pins.

Remember that you can also turn a waist wrap around so that the bow is at the back.

How to Choose, Style, and Wear Scarves

With literally hundreds of styles to choose from, a few words about assembling a basic scarf wardrobe are in order. The shapes and sizes that you'll probably want to collect include:

▶ SQUARES. Smaller squares can be tied at the neck, stuffed to brighten a jacket pocket, or used to pull hair back from the head; medium-sized squares can be used as belts or sashs, or worn as headwraps or bandeau tops; larger squares are for wearing around the shoulders; oversized squares can be tied as skirts, wrapped as sarongs, or worn as shawls.

▶ TIES. Narrow, tubular ties and bias ties will accent your blouses and jackets with a nicely tailored flourish. Since floppy ties are an eye-catching accessory, they must be

Wrapping It Up

When trying on scarves, tie them in a number of ways to make sure that the fabric hangs properly.

carefully tied so that they hang fluidly. Only buy silk scarves for your work wardrobe. Synthetics invariably hang the wrong way or have a dull finish that is less than fashionable and professional looking.

▶ OBLONGS. Narrow oblongs are especially good for wrapping around the neck in a sleek, collared look. They're also the right shape for wearing as ascots. Larger oblongs work well as shoulder wraps.

Whatever the fabric of your scarf, it should be soft, smooth, and easy to drape. To test a scarf's suppleness and line, hold it by one corner to see how it falls. Another way to be sure that you are buying only the best fabrics is to try knotting two ends of the scarf. If they tie in a graceful knot, you've got a scarf that handles easily. If there's any awkwardness, the scarf will probably never look right, no matter how you style it.

CLASSIC SCARF-STYLE SUGGESTIONS

A work wardrobe of classic skirts and pantsuits would include paisley silk scarves, long, floppy ties, and solid-coloured floppy ties and scarves. Thin stripes and tiny plaids are also recommended, as are small polka dots, pinstripes, plaids, horizontal stripes, and diagonal stripes. Be advised that the smaller the scarf, the smaller the pattern should be. Avoid large patterns that are best suited to large head scarves or shawls.

If you like scarves, the options open to you for both daytime and evening dressing are practically limitless. You can tie cotton and silk scarves like cowboy bandannas, or you can wear two identically styled scarves in contrasting colours. You can combine ornate, lacy scarves with menswear-styled outfits to achieve unusual impact. But this is just the beginning. Here are more ideas for you:

▶ IF YOU wear tweedy jackets, offset their texture and pattern by wearing an ascot in a lushly patterned paisley, plaid, or floral print. To tie an ascot, fold a square scarf into an oblong to make it easier to wrap. Knot it around your neck once. Flip one end over the other and spread both ends so that they look full. Tuck the ends into the neckline of a button-down shirt, and your ascot will add a dash of colourful, classic style.

▶ FOR A wrapped, collarlike scarf, fold a square scarf on the bias. Starting in the front, wrap the scarf twice around your neck. Pull the ends around to the front. Flip the ends over one another and tie in the front, or at the side if you prefer.

▶ FOR AN artful, off-to-the-side neck scarf, fold a long scarf into an oblong and then in half. Take the folded end in one hand, the two loose ends in the other, and place the middle of the scarf at the back of the neck. Now, pull the two ends through the loop of the folded end. To complete the knot, pull ends in the opposite direction until the scarf ties comfortably around your neck—it should be a semisnug fit.

▶ IF YOU happen to own a few long, narrow scarves and would like to tie them a la men's neckties, here's how. Place the scarf under your shirt collar or blouse so that the left end is shorter than the right. Now wrap the right end twice around the left at the top near the collar. Pull the long end up through the V-shape at the top of the tie, then down through the loop made by the two wraps. With your left hand holding the left end of the tie, push the knot up toward the neckline with your right hand until it is tight or where you want it. In this way, you can tie tubular or bias-cut scarves and ties, even thin crocheted scarves.

▶ IF YOU have a favorite pair of gloves or shoes, why not get a scarf in a matching colour—either solid or print—to accent your total look? A fringed scarf tossed over one shoulder would be especially eye-catching.

▶ FOR MAXIMUM warmth, colour, and texture, take two or three oversized oblong scarves and lay them on top of one another. Wrap them twice around your neck, knot them, and let the ends fall naturally. The best fabrics for this kind of wrapping are gauzy cotton or textured fabrics. Cotton and linen knits also work well.

▶ WOOL SCARVES can be saved from the winter doldrums by layering one on top of another as well. Take a long oblong scarf and fold it in half, lengthwise. Start from the front and wrap the ends around your neck, cross them in back, and bring them over your shoulders in front. Now take an identically sized oblong scarf and wrap it around your neck the same way. In the end you've got more colour, more texture, and an individualized scarf style.

▶ IF YOU love wool challis floral scarves—also called peasant scarves—take two differently coloured ones and wrap them around your shoulders for a lush, feminine, European look.

▶ FOR A relaxed, Western-wear look, fold a large, square scarf into a triangle. Place it low under your collarbone with the point towards the side, at an angle. Tie the ends over the opposite shoulder.

▶ TRY THIS variation on the ascot with a long, oblong scarf. Start from the front and wrap it twice around your neck, bringing the ends back around to the front. Cross the ends, flip the top end under, then over the loop. Push the fabric up to make the loop secure and shapely.

▶ FOR A big-knotted look, fold a large square scarf into a triangle. Place it on your shoulders with the point in back. Bring the right end over the left and tie; then bring

Use contrasting scarves to play up the patterns of your clothes.

Get your hair out of your face with a lushly coloured head wrap. You've got a look that's tailormade for a day at the beach, a museum expedition, or a hard day's night.

the left end over the right and tie. Adjust the knot in front so that it's secure. You also can wear this style with the knot in back.

HEAD WRAPS AND HAIR WRAPS

▶ FOR A casually chic head wrap, fold a medium-sized square into a triangle. Place it on your head so that both ends crisscross over the one ear. Next, twist one end tightly. Coil it around the knot and tuck in the end. Now, do the same thing with the other end. To keep the resulting rosette in place, use two bobby pins underneath.

▶ TO MAKE a medium-sized square into a turban, fold it into a triangle. Place the scarf on your head with the point of the triangle in back. Cross the ends over the point. Bring the ends back up to the front and knot them above the edge of the scarf. Tuck them in neatly.

▶ FOR AN ethnic or gypsy-style headwrap, fold a medium-sized scarf into a triangle. Place it on your head so the front covers most of your forehead and the point of the triangle falls over the top of your head and down the back. Now pull the ends back and knot them over the point of the triangle. Let the ends fall freely.

▶ FOR A wide head wrap to hold back your hair, place a large oblong scarf just above your eyebrows. Wrap it around your head to the back. Cross the ends and bring them together toward the front. Knot it on the side.

▶ FOR A sleeker head wrap, fold an oblong or square scarf on the bias. Smooth your hair back behind your ears. Place the scarf under your hair in back and bring the ends to the front, knotting them low on the forehead. Now twist the loose ends tightly and tuck them under the sides of the wrap.

▶ FOR AN attractive bow in the hair, a bias-cut silk scarf can be wrapped around your head and then tied at the side. If the bow is too long and floppy, try wrapping the scarf around your head twice. If there's not enough material, simply double knot the scarf ends.

How to Fluff a Pocket Square into Place

Fold a small square scarf into an oblong then in half lengthwise. Tuck it into the pocket and fluff out the material that emerges from the pocket into draped folds. Hint: Silk is the best material for this style.

Summer Body Wraps

▶ FOR WRAPPING up at the beach after a swim, take a large square and, holding it horizontally, place it across your back. Bring the ends under your arms so that they join in front. Tie a secure knot in the center and you've got a *pareo*, standard attire in the South Seas!

▶ TO MAKE a sinuous sarong skirt, take a large square and hold it horizontally behind you at the waist. Bring the ends to the front and tie a bow at the waist. If you have a brooch that matches the scarf material, you might want to fasten it at the bow.

Evening Scarves

Your festive evening wear may run the gamut from subdued black and white separates to free-spirited fashions exuding up-to-the-minute chic. The finishing touches for dressy or formal evening outfits may be a trifle intimidating, though, if you're on a limited budget. This is why scarves can provide an essentially fashionable missing link as a colourful or textural accent, a formally tied flourish, or a one-of-a-kind art object. The appropriately coordinated scarf can elevate your evening wear to *de luxe* status. A few tried and true examples include:

▶ STRAIGHT, NARROW, finely fringed, white silk scarves have been topping tuxedos for decades as part of the classic evening wear

Handwoven yarns are beautiful to behold, extremely soft, and the warmest wraps for chilly weather.

ensemble for men and women alike. Drape one casually around your neck and let it fly, or try wearing it as an ascot with a dressy blouse and/or jacket that has a classic open neckline.

▶ DARK-HUED, RICH paisley scarves in black, burgundy, or navy are another style that embellishes most evening clothes. For extra flair, look for one with delicate fringed ends.

▶ THIN SILK or rayon scarves shot through with metallic threads in striped or patterned designs will add flash and dash to an evening look.

▶ HANDPAINTED SCARVES with metallic threads in Oriental designs, abstracts, or figurative prints may be rather expensive, but they qualify as "artwear"—simple, elegant, enduring, and unique.

Some more unusual dressy scarf ideas are:

▶ FINELY KNIT raw silk or crocheted linen scarves can be tied any number of ways. The textural element they add to your outfit make them very versatile.

▶ GOLD OR silver metal mesh scarves are very glamourous and are perfect for dressy parties or discotheques. Keep an eye out for handpainted ones for extra special style.

▶ THIN, CRUSHED velvet scarves in opulent, nighttime colours like violet, emerald green, rich red, and royal blue can dress up a plain black suit, dress, or other classic daytime ensemble.

▶ STUDDED SCARVES sprinkled with rhinestones or faux gem studs are another fashion extra that can make almost any outfit suitable for night.

It's a given that designer boutiques in department stores offer the nicest selection of scarves for evening wear, but other venues worth trying are thrift shops, flea markets, antique stores, and vintage clothiers. Also investigate import boutiques: Indian, Guatemalan, and Mexican scarves are often quite ornamental and suitable for daytime *and* evening dressing. Guatemalan goods in particular are quite beautifully crafted, with excellent fabrics and embroidered details.

The flamboyant flutter of a scarf in the breeze never fails to draw appreciative glances.

Gloves, Mittens, and Gauntlets

Once a fixture of all genteel day and evening wardrobes, gloves are now less an essential accessory than an option, except during the winter months. The minimum number of pairs you'll need is: one set of knitted wool gloves (or mittens, which are warmer); one set of classic wrist-length leather ones in black; a pair of dress gloves for special occasions; and some sports gloves to protect your hands during athletic workouts. Whatever the style of gloves, always look for quality before you buy. Check to make sure seams and cuffs are well-stitched, that they

fit properly—an ample fit that allows you to clench your fist and spread your fingers apart—and, of course, that they are made of durable materials. Like shoes and boots, gloves take a considerable amount of abuse from the elements and day-to-day wear, so buy the best you can afford.

CASUAL AUTUMN AND WINTER GLOVE STYLES

Perhaps the best buy in winter gloves is hand-knit wool gloves or mittens from Scotland, Ireland, Norway, or Peru. The wools from these countries are usually water-repellant because they have not been stripped of the natural sheep oils. Additionally, handcrafted gloves are often dyed with long-lasting vegetable dyes. Look for gloves like these in department stores, ski shops, camping outfitters, and import stores. If folkloric patterns appeal to you, Peruvian gloves in particular are known for their vibrant colours and figurative designs. Although they are somewhat hard to come by, small boutiques and flea markets often sell them.

Many women's wear manufacturers present fully coordinated lines of knit outerwear. Choose gloves that match or contrast with scarves and hats as you like. If your favorite material is angora, for instance, select gloves in the colour you prefer and also pick up a matching angora beret. You can also mix or match patterns and textures in gloves, scarves, and hats when you buy from a coordinated designer line.

One slightly unusual glove style that nevertheless happens to be very practical for fall and winter is fingerless gloves, which keep your hands and wrists warm, but leave your fingertips exposed and free to grip a steering wheel or go through a change purse more easily. The bother of tugging off gloves every time you need to use your hands is eliminated. If you want to show off your carefully manicured nails, lacy fingerless gloves are the romantic thing to wear when going out in the evening.

If you have a passion for coordinated accessories, a combination like this one strikes the right balance between warmth and style.

CLASSIC AUTUMN AND WINTER GLOVES

Besides coordinating your gloves with your winter coat, hats, and scarves, have a pair or two of leather gloves to match your shoes, briefcase, or handbags. Thin, unlined black leather gloves are an undeniable classic; whether yours are wrist-length or longer depends on your taste and budget. If you're unduly sensitive to cold weather, perhaps you should find some cashmere- or rabbit fur-lined gloves that are mid-forearm length.

Should you want to use gloves as a colourful accent to your wardrobe, there are unadorned leather gloves in bright hues. A typical department store's glove counter will carry bright leather gloves in most of the primary colours.

For maximum warmth and elegant comfort, cashmere gloves are unrivaled. Cashmere's smooth texture looks good with all cold-weather coat styles and materials—leather, down, wool, or even fake fur. Although cashmere is more costly than most wools, it is appreciably softer, less irritating to the skin, and a little more stylish.

Sports gloves, like specially absorbent cotton ones, prevent your hands from chapping when you jog in cold weather. Down-filled, waterproof gloves can be worn to keep your hands warm during long walks.

Caring for Wool and Knit Gloves

Never take your gloves to a dry cleaner; the chemicals used can weaken the fibers, causing the gloves to wear out prematurely. Instead, wash wool and combination knit gloves in cold water with a mild detergent. After you rinse the gloves in cold water, press one glove at a time between two towels to dry out the fabric.

Never wring the water out of wool gloves and knits—this stretches the fabric out of shape and might make the gloves unwearable. Place gloves on a dry towel away from a heat source and leave them to dry. This cleaning method also applies to wool and combination knit scarves, socks, sweaters, hats, and shawls.

SPECIAL GLOVES FOR DRESSY OCCASIONS

Black leather gloves with a thin lining that come to mid-forearm are a classic choice and a worthwhile investment for evening wear. But if you have a taste for ornamental glamour, there are dozens of dressy evening glove styles to go on the town with. Just a few are:

▶ BLACK GLOVES in a tight-fitting knit fabric, studded with rhinestones or sewn with tiny sequins, pearls, or black beads.

▶ FEATHERWEIGHT, LONG woven gloves shot with Lurex metallic threads; silver or gold would be the most versatile.

▶ WHITE LEATHER "opera" gloves festooned with tiny pearls or white beads that come to mid-forearm.

▶ LONG LACE gloves in white or black. For vampy allure, try fingerless lace gloves.

▶ CROCHETED WRIST-LENGTH or longer black or white gloves.

▶ EXTRA-THIN FELT gloves in black or white. Wrist-length ones with beaded detailing can be very nice.

▶ GAUNTLETS COME in a wide range of styles. The most common is a standard leather glove with flaring cuffs. Another is a fingerless knit or crocheted glove with a cuff that runs to mid-forearm or elbow. White or black leather gauntlets that flare round the wrist add drama to any evening outfit. For all-out glamour, you might want to wear fingerless, crocheted Lurex gauntlets that stop at the elbow. Beaded, studded, or sequined gauntlets add flash to a festive outfit; everyone will want to shake hands with you!

Antique clothing stores and flea markets are good sources for distinctive, dressy gloves. It's fairly common to find vintage, *haute couture* gloves for very little in a recycled clothing store. Estate sales, variety stores, and discount retail outlets are also not to be overlooked.

BUDGET GLOVE IDEAS

If there's a will, there's a way, so if you want to supplement your collection of gloves without spending much, here are some surefire suggestions:

▶ THE MOST inexpensive, rugged, cold-weather gloves are leather work gloves, available at household supply stores, work clothes shops, and gardening stores. They'll probably last a lifetime. Perfect with jeans and basic casual wear, work gloves come in beige, brown, and orange.

▶ PLAIN WHITE cotton gloves can be

custom-dyed at home in your favorite shades. You could also hand-paint them or sew on trimmings at the wrist. The final effect can give you a designer look at homemade prices. All you really need is imagination and an hour or two for creation!

▶ WHEN WOOL or combination knit gloves wear out at the fingertips, don't throw them away. Instead, cut off the tips, fold the fabric over and sew around each tip so that you have a brand new pair of fingerless gloves. If your gloves are black or navy, you might even want to use metallic thread for a jazzy, evening-style seam.

Although leather gloves are the obvious accessory to a leather jacket, use colourful wool gloves to key into the colour scheme of your clothing.

DRESSING RIGHT FOR DAY & NIGHT

CHAPTER EIGHT:

Every year, every week, every day, there are special occasions where the way you dress is of key importance. If it's a business meeting or lunch, you'll want to convey a professional image to those you are working with. And if it's a social occasion, such as a small formal dinner party or a night at the ballet, you'll want to look comfortably elegant in what you wear. After all, when you are dressed appropriately, no matter what the occasion, you'll feel your best because you look your best.

If you've assembled your basic wardrobe with care, however, you won't have to buy new clothing every time a special occasion arises. Rely on your collection of accessories to give you the perfect look and put you in the right mood for the event. Here are dress ideas and suggestions for all kinds of notable occasions, from a job interview or an office party to a business trip or a night at a disco.

How to Dress for Special Work-Related Occasions

In the professional world, your clothing and accessories are vitally important to the overall impression that others form about you. This happens to be especially true in the case of job interviews, business lunches, meetings, and office parties. These are all delicate situations where discretion with your dress can help enhance your professional image.

JOB INTERVIEWS

In the case of job interviews, do some research into the firm you're applying to before you decide on what to wear for the appointment. If the company is in a conservative business, choose an outfit in keeping with the nature of the company. This advice applies both to entry level job seekers and aspiring executives; no matter what your position, you must dress carefully, with a certain amount of authority and consideration for the company's identity.

In most cases, a simply tailored suit—without details—would be your best bet. If you prefer structured clothing, choose a suit with lightly padded shoulders. Avoid boxy, exaggerated shoulder pads; their overt styling might be too fashionable for the interviewer to take you seriously. A streamlined, classic blouse in a natural fiber (cotton, silk, or linen, for example) is the thing to wear with your suit. Select pantyhose in a fairly neutral colour. Semi-opaques in bone, navy, or black would probably be most appropriate. As for your footwear, low-heeled pumps in an understated style and colour—black, navy, or brown—coordinated with your suit are recommended. Jewellery should be kept to a minimum. Save your dangling earrings for another occasion and stick with studs; leave decorative rings and bracelets at home and go with just a wristwatch. If you happen to have a single strand of pearls in a medium length, these would be perfectly appropriate accessories for a job interview. Anything longer than this will look too showy for the occasion. Now that you've got your look together, it's up to you to complete the ensemble with a handbag or briefcase that matches your shoes.

If you're applying to the sort of company that is relatively free from the conventions of dress, add a little innovation and individuality to the straightforward, classic suit ensemble look. "Innovation" means anything from adding some special antique jewellery, such as a wristwatch, cuff links, or earrings to an elegant blouse/blazer/skirt ensemble to combining a houndstooth-checked blazer with black wool pants and sleek, black leather flats. Try to find out how people at all levels of the company dress before you assemble your outfit and accessories. A quick telephone call to the company's receptionist might be in order; explain that you're trying to get an idea of what the office wardrobe style is like so you'll be suitably attired for the interview. But be careful to always dress so you'll feel comfortable, self-confident, and assured.

BUSINESS MEETINGS

For important meetings with colleagues or clients at the office or in a restaurant, common sense dictates that you "dress for success." Your total look should convey an assured professionalism; clothing and accessories should signal your mastery of the business world and your career. Never dress deliberately to show status or to intimidate others. The secret is to put together outfits that are well-tailored to your business environment but that look stylish and unique. Some suggestions for brightening staid "corporate" clothes are:

▶ GIVE A severely tailored business suit and a button-down blouse some flair with a colourful silk scarf tied ascot-style. Or wear a silver or gold bar pin on the lapel of the suit. Pocket scarves are another good accessory choice for a simple suit.

▶ DRAMATIZE SERIOUS suits and dresses with shoes that add a colourful or textural accent to your clothing. One example is lizard-skin or suede pumps or spectators with black patent-leather toes and bone-coloured leather vamp and slingback straps. As far as colours go, match a pair of leather pumps in deep mauve with a gray flannel suit. Wine-coloured lizard-skin and suede pumps would liven up your black dresses and separates; if you are nervous that some colours might be too bright, it's better to err on the side of subtlety. You don't want to draw too much attention to yourself in a business situation.

▶ EMPHASIZE THE texture of a classically cut linen suit with a ribbed or cable-knit short-sleeved cotton sweater. Try a narrow, woven leather belt; its texture will enhance that of the linen.

▶ ACCENT YOUR conservative clothes with bold but tasteful jewellery such as wide gold bangle bracelets or large pins or brooches worn at the collar of your blouses or on the lapel of your jacket. A large-faced, subtly decorative wristwatch will also add some stylish impact to your total look.

Dressing Right for Day & Night • 131

Avoid the look of a corporate clone by carefully but uniquely accessorizing a tailored outfit. In this case, a white dress is complemented by a spirited jacket, scarf, belt, handbag, jewellery, and shoes.

▶ ADD INTEREST to the all-too-familiar look of a jacket-and-skirt suit with the addition of vertical ribbed or other subtly textured pantyhose.

OFFICE PARTIES

Always pay attention to subtlety when putting together an outfit for an office party. Instead of seasonal trends or personal preferences, the setting and nature of the party should be the deciding factor behind your choice of clothing and accessories. For example, if the event is to be a late afternoon or early evening cocktail party, you'll look most appropriate in the sort of clothing and accessories that you regularly wear to work. You might want to add some colourful earrings, a silver or gold necklace, or a semiformal belt to your ensemble, but keep it simple, since this is, after all, a work-related occasion.

If you'll be going directly to the party after work, here are some suggestions for sprucing up your daytime look:

▶ ON THE day of the party, bring along a dressy sweater (cashmere or angora) to wear on top of a gray suit skirt. Leave your suit jacket in your office and dress up the sweater with a strand of pearls or a pendant necklace and matching earrings.

▶ IF YOU often dress in tailored pants, jacket, and blouse ensembles, wear a typical workday outfit and bring a dressy scarf and belt to play up your look for the party. Because the belt will be your focal accessory, keep your jewellery simple and in proportion with the belt's width and buckle.

For day-into-night dressing, crystal jewellery will awaken any dark-coloured outfit with sparkling drama.

▶ IF THE party is to be held in a restaurant, a basic black dress, with or without a matching jacket, would be a tasteful choice. Some dressy black shoes—flats or pumps—would complement your look, but high heels are definitely *not* the thing to wear—they're just too dressy. Again, it's advisable to keep your jewellery understated; a few pieces, such as earrings, a wristwatch, and a necklace, will suffice. Or, if you have a belt with a decorative buckle, balance it with some simple earrings.

Business trips

Your company is sending you out of town to clinch an important business deal; or you've been asked to speak at a national convention of people in your industry; or you're going to an elite seminar session for those in your field. Any of these business trip scenarios is becoming more and more commonplace for women who are advancing in their fields. If you're not entirely certain about the clothes to take, this uncertainty might adversely affect your performance during the business trip. Here are some general guidelines to help you pack efficiently for a typical three-day business trip.

First of all, as a representative of your company, you should be professionally attired even while traveling to appointments. The person in the airplane seat next to you just may be an executive from another branch of your corporation or a competitor in your field. Because you never know whom you'll meet, it's wise to wear a tailored blazer and skirt or a suit when you're "on the road." Pick a classic blouse to wear with your suit or separates and bring a handbag that matches your shoes, and briefcase.

It's a good idea to pack a tailored dress and matching jacket for dinner engagements. Whether it's a dress in basic black or one in a print, it's got to be discreet enough to suit a professional situation. Wear it with semiconservative black pumps and natural or bone-coloured pantyhose.

Your proper professional image should be of paramount concern to you for it makes a statement as distinctly as any corporate memo. Plan your outfits with the same zeal you bring to your work.

Besides the suit you wear in transit, pack another in your suitcase. You can vary the look of a suit with several blouses, so you only need two suits for three days of meetings. For a key daytime discussion group, meeting, or lecture, you'll want to wear your "dress for success" clothes. Perhaps an impeccable silk shirt with one of your suits would be the most advisable look.

Accessorize the look with a floppy bow tie in a classic paisley pattern or maybe just a string of pearls. It all depends on how businesslike you want to appear and what sort of clothing will make you feel most comfortable. If this means wearing a black pin-striped suit with a cream silk shirt that comes with its own bow and ties in a flourish, then wear it! An outfit like this is neat and coolly professional, but feminine and classic. Black pumps and semi-sheer pantyhose would complete the ensemble.

One mark of a smart traveller is her contingency packing plan—specifically, the extras she packs just in case something rips or

This outfit is a study in chic, semiformal dressing.

stains. Bring along two extra blouses to go with your suits, even though you may not need them. Two extra pairs of pantyhose tucked into your suitcase will come in handy if you happen to snag the ones you're wearing. An extra scarf or two and a small sewing kit ought to take care of any other clothing complications.

Bring along a camisole to wear under your dress or with one of your suit skirts. For flawless evening dressing, a short jacket or dressy cardigan sweater to top your dress would be another on-the-road asset.

Casual to Semiformal Dressing

With the resurgence in popularity of daytime parties such as brunch and afternoon cocktails, women often find themselves puzzling over what to wear. If the invitation reads "casual," or the hostess tells you to dress "semiformal," how do you interpret these instructions? Here are style suggestions for this mysterious category of daytime dressing—casual to semiformal:

▶ PANTS, EITHER as part of a suit or separately, offer one solution to what to wear for daytime occasions. If it's a casual gathering, jeans, a tailored blouse and a wool tweed blazer will do just fine. Wear this outfit with leather flats and a matching leather belt. For spring and summer, or between-season weather, substitute the wool blazer with a linen jacket or a stylish denim one. Go ahead and accessorize with whatever earrings, bracelets, and rings, you feel comfortable in. For a semiformal party, a tailored jacket, dressy pants, and a pretty sweater or blouse would be in order. For instance, a finely tailored, wool knit blazer with built-in shoulder pads could be worn over a crisp white cotton, tuxedo-style shirt and black velvet pants. This admittedly, is a winter outfit, but the same kind of plan would work for warmer weather, too.

▶ A GOOD outfit for summer semiformal dressing? Try a pale pink, raw silk blazer over a sleeveless gray linen blouse. Wear a string of pearls and pearl stud earrings to fulfill the semiformal requirements. White cotton pleated pants with lacy hose underneath would dress up your bottom half. As for shoes, how about some dressy, pink, leather, medium-heeled pumps? A pale pink bone coloured leather belt with a gold buckle would be another attractive, semiformal touch for your outfit.

▶ IF YOU happen to prefer dresses and skirts to pants, then you have a bit more flexibility when dressing for casual and semiformal occasions. Because skirts and dresses are ultra-classic female garb worn with pantyhose and dressy shoes, all you have to do is isolate the style, colour, and fabric appropriate for the specific season and occasion. One example is an above-the-knee, black leather skirt worn with an emerald green, softly draped satin blouse. Accessorize this outfit with sheer black hose, green lizard-skin and leather pumps, and antique gold earrings, bracelets, and rings. This ensemble would look smashing at a late afternoon cocktail party, an art gallery opening, or a dinner party, but it's much too chic for a noontime brunch, even a semiformal one. For a semiformal daytime occasion, wear the black leather skirt with a white lace blouse, textured white pantyhose or sheers in white or bone, and black patent-leather tuxedo pumps. The gold antique jewellery, more distinctive-looking than most costume jewellery, would be in keeping with the occasion and the outfit.

Dress in sleek style for most semiformal occasions to be de luxe *without being* de trop.

Go all out for evening glamour with jewellery that echoes the exuberance of your garments.

▶ CASUAL SKIRT and dress ensembles can be built around denim skirts; wool jersey dresses; seersucker jackets and skirts; or cotton, wool and cashmere sweaters, any of which can be paired with classic shoes and boots. The overall impression of the outfit should be stylistically consistent, rather than impeccably coordinated. For example, a gray cashmere sweater with a long blue denim skirt and low-heeled gray suede boots would be a comfortably casual outfit for brunch or a casual afternoon gathering.

Dressing for Semiformal Evening Occasions

Sit-down dinners, cocktail parties, dinner dates, and disco dancing are a few typical semiformal evening occasions to which you could wear the same classic garment—your basic black dress. Select your shoes, jewellery, scarves, and handbag to complement the line, style, fabric, and details of the dress, but keep the specific occasion in mind as well. Here are some representative basic black dresses in different styles and fabrics and ideas for dressing them up.

▶ A LONG-SLEEVED tailored silk dress that stops just above the knee and comes with a matching silk sash that ties at the waist would look terrific with black suede pumps and sheer black hose, silver and crystal earrings, and silver bracelets. A black suede clutch would finish off this evening look, and you could add black suede gloves, if that's your style. The total look of this dress with accessories is best suited for occasions such as intimate dinners, festive cocktail parties, and sit-down dinner parties at a business associate or friend's house.

▶ A SCOOP-NECKED, short-sleeved velvet dress that flares to about mid-calf length needs high-heeled black patent-leather pumps or, for extra glamour, black satin high heels. Go for textured sheer black pantyhose—perhaps with delicate rhinestone-studded seams—sheer, silvery gray or bone stockings, or intricate black or white lace hose. Pearl jewellery make black velvet *de luxe;* rhinestone pieces mixed with pearls are even more dazzling. A black velvet, satin, or patent-leather purse on a thin shoulder strap would be perfect with this outfit. An ensemble such as this will carry you in style to the ballet or theatre, to New Year's Eve celebrations, and to special dress-up gatherings with family or friends.

▶ A SLEEVELESS, simply cut, knee-length, black cotton knit sheath with slits at the sides becomes sophisticated with a black snakeskin belt or any brightly coloured belt at the waist. A dressy belt adds decorative impact, but also hitches up the hemline to a racy, almost mini-skirt length. Coordinate your pumps or high heels with the belt's colour or texture. For instance, a silver-studded, black leather belt would be the centerpiece of your outfit, so match it up with black leather pumps or heels, rather than detracting from it with any old pair of dressy shoes. A jazzy outfit like this is tailor-made for exciting nights out on the town: disco dancing at the clubs, festive parties, or rock concerts, for example.

Dressing Right for Day & Night • 137

***The basic black dress springs into action: use your imagination
and fancy with hosiery, shoe, and jewellery choices.***

Depending on your choice of accessories, you can present yourself as a downtown diva, a frothy party girl, a femme fatale, or a goddess in white.

Dressing Right for Day & Night • 139

Elegant gloves cloak your hands in exquisite mystery while drawing attention to the pretty bracelets encircling your wrists.

Basic Black for a Black-Tie Affair

Stylistically, black-tie events hover between the fashion categories of semiformal and white-tie (very formal) occasions. Should you ever be invited to a black-tie gala, sprucing up your black dress with a glamourous black jacket would be entirely appropriate for the event. Here are some examples.

▶ A STRAPLESS black dinner dress with a fitted, black satin or velvet jacket on top is a classic black-tie outfit. The jacket, however, must have some dressy details such as shoulder pads or big, puffy sleeves, to qualify for black-tie stature. A satin, tuxedo-style jacket with sleeves rolled up to expose a wristful of bracelets is a good look; add earrings, necklaces, and rings for even more black-tie chic.

▶ EMBROIDERED AND jewelled jackets over knee-length, semiformal black dresses make an extravagant statement very much in the spirit of black-tie events. A black velvet, multicolour sequined jacket, for instance, can be further enhanced by real or faux gemstone jewellery in shades that match the sequins. Bright, glittery earrings, jewelled hair combs, bracelets—any or all of these do justice to a decorative jacket.

▶ IF YOU prefer big, bold jewellery, go with just an ornate brooch on the lapel or in the collarbone area of a tailored, black jacket. In some dress-up situations, less is definitely more—more stylish, more elegant, more striking.

▶ ANOTHER ACCESSORY that can dramatize any dressy or black-tie outfit is a high-style evening shoe or sandal. Silver or gold high-heeled sandals with lots of narrow straps across the vamp and an ankle strap are a timeless sort of style that can be worn with long or short dresses or dressy pants. Other sorts of "accent" shoes would be beaded, sequined, or studded styles played up with festively coloured belts, earrings, gloves, bracelets, or handbags. Experiment and mix coordinates until you arrive at a well-balanced, eye catching ensemble that looks utterly correct from head to toe. If you feel comfortable in it, then this is a good sign that you can carry it off in public. If you doubt any part of your outfit, rethink your ensemble and try again.

Black tie dressing is the ultimate in studied, traditional elegance.

Accessorizing Other Formal Clothes for Specific Occasions

Afternoon weddings and formal dances or dinners are very significant events on your social calendar. These are gatherings where impeccable attire, tasteful accessories, and neat grooming are of vital importance. Put yourself together carefully using these suggestions and tips, and you'll feel appropriately dressed for the occasion.

▶ FOR AN afternoon wedding, no matter what your style of dress, there are a few basic accessories that you'll want to consider: classic, understated jewellery, such as a strand of pearls; gemstone or pearl earrings; a small, dressy shoulder bag or clutch; pastel-coloured or white lacy gloves. Medium-heeled shoes that are not ostentatious and a subdued silk scarf are also advisable accessories. Because it's poor etiquette to wear anything which might upstage the bride, keep your makeup low-key and understated; strive for sophistication—not flashiness.

▶ EVENING WEDDINGS are another story—you can dress to the proverbial nines. If you feel like wearing a sequined strapless dress, metallic gold pumps, elbow-length black gloves, and faux pearl-studded hair combs, then go ahead. An elegant little purse, such as a *minaudiere*, is the thing to carry. Top the dress with a tailored jacket and a tiny hat for maximum style. But be sure it has no veil; leave that for the bride to wear!

▶ ALTHOUGH YOU might not wear a bona fide ball gown to a formal dinner or dance, you'll still want to dress in black-tie style for this occasion. Typical formal wear accessories would include: black satin pumps (they're more elegant than patent-leather); white satin or fine-lace elbow-length gloves, and well-made, precious jewellery. If you don't own any real gold, pearls, or gemstones, high-quality costume pieces will do. When choosing jewellery, however, realize that whether it's real or costume, the pieces must be appropriate for the occasion. It's just as important to avoid jewellery that makes you look *underdressed* as it is to wear pieces that make you appear overdressed. For formal occasions, discretion is the key.

▶ SUITABLE ACCESSORIES for a black-tie-style dress would be pearl-and-diamond or pearl-and-rhinestone earrings, a strand of pearls around your neck, and a pair of white lace gloves. Never wear bangles with gloves, as the bracelets get caught in the fabric and the proportions often look awkward. If you want to wear some decor at your wrist, wear a pearl cuff bracelet. The wrong sort of look for a black-tie dress would be silver hoop earrings with a silver-and-turquoise necklace and a silver cuff bracelet. These accessories are simply too casual, too heavy and, therefore, inappropriate for a black-tie event.

A festive evening purse, such as the **minaudière** *in the photo, is the finishing touch for formal accessorizing.*

Dressing Up at Home

What you wear to your own party is a matter of personal preference, which depends on the time it is to take place and the formality of the occasion. For brunches, cocktail parties, and buffet-style dinner parties, dressy pants and a silk blouse or stylish sweater with leather flats might be just right; add pizzazz with minimal jewellery and, perhaps, a scarf around your neck. Those with a flair for pageantry might wear a few outstanding accessories for festivity's sake. Even if you're planning to wear jeans and a T-shirt, designer Keni Valenti advises you to dress them up. "Wear bold, sparkling jewellery, unusually decorated belts, bright-coloured shoes... all the things you never get to wear to other people's parties! Be adventurous, and make your outfit something special. Your guests will enjoy the party more," he insists.

For an old fashioned, sit-down dinner party, a semiformal short dress with patterned pantyhose (lace, for example, or tiny metallic geometrics on black) and dressy pumps could be enhanced by dramatic earrings, bracelets, and rings.

Remember that the fabric of your dress can set the tone of your outfit and accessories. Brocades, velvets, silks, wool jerseys, leather, and suede are all beautifully made, rich fabrics that look even more so when dressed up with the right accessories. Brocades, velvets, and silks, for example, look very glamourous with lacy pantyhose, black leather pumps, and sparkling real or costume jewellery. Wool jerseys, leathers, and suedes are enhanced by sheer pantyhose, leather or suede pumps, and bright gold or sterling silver earrings, chain necklaces, and bracelets or bangles.

Dazzling costume jewellery will make staid separates suitable for gala events.

Vintage garments often give you a costumed aura, just the thing to wear for a garden party, a summer wedding, or an alfresco meal.

Touches from the Past

Embroidered camisoles, fringed, handwoven floral-print shawls, romantic Victorian jewellery, and chunky, imitation crocodile handbags are examples of ever-fresh "vintage" accessories—distinctive pieces from bygone eras that can be used to great effect by the innovative dresser. For example, if you combined the items mentioned above with a pair of jeans, you'd pay homage to a parade of fashion moments: the camisole from the 1930s; the fringed shawl from the 1920s; the Victorian rings or jewellery from the late nineteenth century, and the imitation crocodile handbag a paragon of 1950s chic! Admittedly, pulling this outfit together takes a certain savvy that some of us may lack, but vintage accessories, especially jewellery, are a delightful and affordable route to dressing with individuality and charm.

Pearl drop earrings from the 1930s, for instance, add discreet glamour to the simplest black dress. Wear them with a strand of contemporary faux pearls and the result will be a subtle mix of styles that looks perfectly in sync.

There's no end to the design possibilities you can try with various belts, shoes and gloves from past eras. When you combine vintage pieces with modern ones, the effects can be surprisingly distinctive.

Shawls and scarves are valuable mainstays of between season outfits.

Between Season Dressing

Dressing for between-season weather can be a bother; the problem is finding clothes that are just the right weight and warmth for variable weather. Layering your outfits with sleeveless wool and cotton vests, cardigan sweaters of light, medium, and heavy weaves, and with scarves and shawls is the most sensible strategy. This way, you can add or subtract garments as need be.

For instance, if you're dressing for spring/summer weather that's still a bit chilly, slip a light, cotton-knit vest over your T-shirt and skirt outfit. Wear pantyhose that are the same shade as the vest to pull the look together. For extra warmth, wear a scarf wrapped around your neck in a colour that matches the vest and hose. You can always remove the scarf or the vest when you get indoors where it's warmer. No matter which garment you remove, you'll still be coordinated in thoughtfully chosen separates. Other accessories that can help you get through seasonal transitions with style are lightweight berets, head wraps, and lightweight leather gloves or cotton and wool fingerless ones.

Keni Valenti recommends that you keep a few spare, between-season accessories in your desk at the office, so you'll be appropriately dressed for lunchtime or evening social engagements. "A scarf, a pair of gloves, and definitely an umbrella will take care of most weather complications," he says. You might also want to stash a pair of rain boots in your bottom drawer.

You can also layer undergarments for comfortable, between-season dressing. The most useful piece is a lightweight, finespun silk camisole. Why? Because silk makes just about the warmest lingerie you can find. And, because it's so thin and light, you can wear it under a blouse or T-shirt on blustery days when you want to look dressed for spring yet be sure you feel warm enough.

Quick-Change Artistry

Many women, like bodybuilder and model Beth Rubino, work in an office all day, then meet up with friends for dinner, dancing, or whatever. Although a busy schedule makes for a stimulating life-style, it nevertheless leaves little, if any, time for coordinating your wardrobe and accessories for a special social engagement. Beth suggests you keep an assortment of accessories, like the following ones, in your office drawer or gym locker for making quick style changes in the evening hours:

▶ A STRAND of white costume pearls.
▶ ONE OR two pairs of dressy earrings.
▶ SOME COLOGNE or perfumed body lotion.
▶ A PAIR of dressy pantyhose.

Of course, you can also tuck into your purse any scarves, clip-on bows for your shoes, hair combs, or other items that you plan to wear after work. Planning ahead will allow you to make a seamless transition from sensible daytime clothes to dressy evening wear in a matter of minutes.

By now you've probably realized how easy it is to coordinate your wardrobe and accessories to maximum effect. All it takes is a few smart purchases and five minutes of planning before you get dressed. Once you decide on what clothes to wear, start choosing the jewellery that will enhance the fabrics of your garments, the scarves that will accent your outfit, the pantyhose that will flatter your legs, the shoes and belt that will pull your look together and so on. Smart accessorizing puts you in control of your total look; it's one of the privileges of being a well-dressed woman.

Change a daytime look into a nighttime ensemble by clipping on a pair of earrings or adding a scarf.

146 • Accessory Chic

The secret to office-to-evening wardrobe transitions? Use a daytime garment, such as this blazer, to form the basis of your nighttime ensemble.

Dressing Right for Day & Night • 147

Untie a bow here, add a scarf there, clamp on a bracelet, and slip into some stiletto heels. Delicate accessory adjustments can shift your look to suit any social or business engagement.

GLOSSARY

Appendix One:

A-Line: An A-line skirt or dress is tailored so that it has an approximate A shape. A clear example of A-line styling would be the dresses that most nurses wear.

All-in-One: Cut like a one piece swimsuit, an all-in-one is a bra and panties together. It moulds your body in a flattering way and is, therefore, good under tight clothing. Some all-in-ones even have built in underwire bras.

Bangles: Generally speaking, this is a bracelet with no clasp that slips on over the hand, such as a silver hoop bracelet.

Bed jacket: A short- or long-sleeved negligée jacket meant for wearing in the boudoir.

Beret: A round, brimless cloth cap worn high on the head. Originated by the Basques in France, today, berets come in a variety of fabrics, such as suede, wool, and velvet.

Bodyhose: A filmy nylon undersuit that covers the body from the bust to the toes.

Boot Liners: Footless wool leggings that cover the area from the ankle to just below the knee.

Broadcloth: A tightly woven cotton, silk, or synthetic blend fabric with a narrow, crosswise stitch. Broadcloth is primarily a shirting fabric.

Brocade: A heavy cotton or silk fabric interwoven with a rich, raised design. Indian craftsmen originated brocade weaving thousands of years before Christ. Popular motifs include birds, vines, and floral bouquets.

Brooch: A large decorative pin or clasp.

Camisole: A woman's sleeveless underbodice, usually made of lightweight material, that stops at the waist.

Cashmere: A fine, soft wool from a cashmere goat; it is also one of the warmest wools. The name is derived from the Himalayan region of Kashmir.

Challis: A lightweight fabric usually printed with a floral or paisley design and made of wool, cotton, or rayon.

Cinnabar: A semi-precious substance made from tree resins and noted for its rich red colour.

Clutch: A small-sized purse that is carried in the hand and usually worn with evening clothes.

Crushed Velvet: Velvet whose texture has been manipulated so as to appear slightly ribbed or "crushed."

Cuff: When referring to clothing, the cuff is the section of sleeve that closes around your wrists or is turned up at the bottom of your pants leg. In jewellery terms, a cuff is usually a wide bracelet without a clasp that fits over your wrist and is worn on the forearm, just above the wrist.

Espadrilles: A sandal or slip-on shoe with canvas uppers and a rope sole.

Evening Sandals: A delicate, thinly strapped shoe, either flat or with heels, that is dressy enough to wear with evening clothes.

Fedora: A soft felt hat with a brim that can be turned up or down and a low crown that is creased lengthwise. Fedoras were originally worn by men, but today they are a very popular style with women as well.

Foulard: A lightweight plain-woven or twill fabric of silk or silk and cotton, usually printed with a tiny design. Ties, scarves, and sashes are readily available in foulard fabric.

Grosgrain: A heavy silk or rayon fabric with narrow, horizontal ribs. Grosgrain ribbons are often used as hatbands.

Head Wrap: Generally speaking, any piece of cloth that is wrapped around the head to hold back the hair. There are many ways—from casual to drop dead elegant—that headwraps can be tied.

High Heels: Any shoes with heels seven centimeters (three inches) or higher.

Hound's Tooth: A small checkered textile design, usually found on wool garments.

Jacquard: An intricately woven pattern resulting in a highly textured fabric, jacquard patterns are often found in silk fabrics. A jacquard motif is often so detailed it resembles an etching or illustration, the fabric somewhat finer than brocade.

Jersey: A soft fabric of wool, cotton, or rayon. Jersey is very comfortable to wear.

Kimono: A long, loose-fitting, wide-sleeved cotton or silk robe, usually worn with a sash. Today, a kimono also means a bathrobe, dress, or dressing gown that is modeled after the classic Japanese garment.

Lace: A delicate silk, cotton, or nylon fabric in an open, weblike weave usually depicting floral blossoms, leaves, or hearts. Usually found as trim on garments and undergarments, lace is also made into scarves, pantyhose, and handkerchiefs.

Lamé: A fabric having thin metal threads woven into it to create a metallic sheen.

Lorgnette: Eyeglasses with a short handle or attached to a chain. They are also known as "opera glasses."

Minaudière: a tiny, hard-cased evening purse made of metal, metal mesh, tortoise shell, or plastic.

Oxford Cloth: A cotton cloth of a tight weave, oxford cloth is primarily used for shirting fabric.

Paisley: Originally, paisley meant a soft, wool fabric printed with a pattern derived from the swirling, palmette motifs of Persian and Indian rugs. Today, paisley is a term used to describe colourful designs of abstract, curvy, Persian/Indian motifs.

Pin Stripes: A kind of fabric, usually dark-coloured, with thin, lighter coloured stripes.

Ramie: A flax-like Asian fiber found in many garments, ramie is quite durable.

Satin: A smooth silk, cotton, nylon, or rayon fabric woven so that it is glossy on one side and dull on the other. Satin is rather expensive and quite fragile and is a popular fabric for lingerie.

Seersucker: A summer weight fabric, generally made of cotton or rayon, with a crinkled surface and a striped pattern. The most common seersucker colour combination is white with a blue stripe.

Slingback: A shoe design characterized by its strap that extends from the covered vamp area to expose the side and heel of the foot. Slingbacks can be flat or heeled.

Spectator: A dressy shoe with toe in a different color leather from the rest of the shoe. A popular spectator style would be a slingback, with a black patent leather toe and a bone leather upper and strap.

Stirrups: Pants or pantyhose with feet cut out and a strap that fits around the middle of the foot.

Studs: Studs are tiny pieces of molded metal, or stones set in metal that are used to decorate fabrics or leathers. On stud earrings the decorative piece is attached to a straight piece of metal that fits through the hole in the earlobe.

Teddy: A delicate undergarment, the teddy is designed like a one piece swimsuit and therefore takes the place of both a bra and underpants.

Turban: Originally a Moslem headdress, a turban is a long scarf that is wrapped around the head to achieve a textural look.

Velvet: Originally made only of silk, velvet is now available in many fibers. Silk and cotton velvets are the most luxurious and well made. Velvet has a short, dense pile and a glossy finish.

Velveteen: Less expensive than velvet, this is a cotton fabric with a short, tight pile that closely resembles velvet.

A Shopper's Guide and Sources

Appendix Two:

There are a few shopping strategies that, once learned, can help you conserve valuable time, money, and energy. Stock up on accessories during department store seasonal sales, for instance. Although sale periods may vary slightly from region to region, generally speaking, the following accessories are usually available at reduced prices at these specific times of the year:

▶ BRAS AND UNDERPANTS: mid-summer and mid-winter.

▶ PANTYHOSE: early autumn and mid-summer.

▶ SOCKS: the tail end of each season.

▶ BATHING SUITS AND BEACHWEAR: early spring, mid-summer, and late summer.

▶ SHOES AND BOOTS: summer shoes at the end of August; autumn shoes in the middle of December; winter boots in the middle of March; spring shoes at the end of June or beginning of July.

▶ BELTS, HATS, GLOVES, AND SCARVES: late winter and late summer. Keep your eyes peeled for special sales during the height of autumn and winter.

▶ JEWELLERY: at the end of each season.

▶ UMBRELLAS: early spring and early autumn.

Get on the mailing lists of department stores near you to keep abreast of upcoming sales. Also read the ad pages of local newspapers to learn of special, one-day, or weekend sales. National holidays are often some of the best sale days. If you can brave the crowds, you'll end up with some great bargains. Ask salespeople what sales are coming up, too.

Discount Shopping: Special Retail Stores

Let's say you're a designer clothes, shoe, and accessory addict. You'll gladly starve for a few weeks to sink your money into high-priced but, nevertheless, valuable and exquisite garments. But have you ever tried shopping in factory outlets, discount chains, or clothing and shoe warehouses? These kinds of retail stores operate along the same basic premise: Price tags are dated, and merchandise discounts increase with time. Some national discount chains, like Sym's, Loehmann's, and Marshall's (see Sources), carry the cream of American fashion designers, as well as foreign-made fashions and accessories. It is not unusual to find Charles Jourdan shoes at less than half price; Cacharel silk scarves for ten dollars; Christian Dior textured pantyhose for pennies. If you long to dress with high-fashion style but assume that it's out of the range of your budget, think again. When you go to the right sources, you can shop every season and pay bargain-basement prices for even the most expensively made fashion accessories and clothing. You might have to make a special effort to get to a factory outlet, but the travel time you spend will be more than compensated by the savings and satisfaction that you gain.

UNITED KINGDOM SOURCES

Department Stores:

C & A
505 Oxford St.,
London W1

Fenwick's
63 New Bond St.,
London W1

Harrod's
87-135 Brompton Rd.,
London SW1

Marks and Spencer
458 Oxford St.,
London W1

Selfridge's and Miss Selfridge's
400 Oxford St.,
London W1

General Accessories:

Artwork
33 St. Christopher's Pl.,
London W1

Bill
93 New Bond St.,
London W1

Blax
11 Sicilian Ave.,
London WC1

Design Gap Shop
2 Hyper Hyper,
Kensington High St.,
London W8

Elle
4 New Bond St.,
London SW3
   and
23 Brompton Rd.,
London SW3

Fiorucci
133 New Bond St.,
London SW1

Hackett
65C New Kings Rd.,
London SW6

Inca
45 Elizabeth St.,
London SW1

Jaeger
204 Regent St.,
London W1

P.X.
57 Endell St.,
London WC2

Whites Clothing Company Limited
31 Jerdan Pl.,
London SW6

Vintage Clothing:

Morley's
85 King's Rd.,
London SW3

Flip
191 King's Rd.,
London SW3
   and
126 Long Acre,
London WC2

Dancewear:

Porselli
9 West St.,
London WC2

Jewellery:

Artifice
16 Portobello Green,
Portobello Rd.,
London W11

Aspects
3-5 Whitfield St.,
London W1

Butler & Wilson
183 Fulham Rd.,
London SW10

Clarissa
20 Gordon Pl.,
London W8

Detail
49 Endell St.,
London WC2

Jane Adam
65 Rothschild Rd.,
London W4

Louise Slater
167 Brick Ln.,
London E2

Marlene McKibbin
15 Sunbury Workshop,
Hocker St.,
London E2

Rocks
15 St. Christophers Pl.,
London W1
    and
2 S. Molton St.,
London W1

Stilo
60 Kensington Market,
Kensington High St.,
London W8

Shoes:

Ad Hoc
396 Kings Rd.,
London SW10

Bertie
48 S. Molton St.,
London W1

    and
15 The Market,
Covent Garden,
London WC2

Derber
80 Kensington High St.,
London W8

Freelance
39 Floral St.,
London WC2

Hobbs
33A Kings Rd.,
London SW3
    and
84 King's Rd.,
London SW3
    and
47 S. Molton St.,
London W1
    and
17 The Market,
Covent Garden,
London WC2

Robot Shoes
39 Floral St.,
London WC2
    and
23 King's Rd.,
London SW10

Trip
12 The Market,
Covent Garden,
London WC2

Hats:

Anne Tomlin Designs
401½ Workshops,
Wandsworth Rd.,
London SW8

Big Apple
19 Hyper Hyper,
Kensington High St.,
London W8
    and
130A Acre Ln.,
Brixton

Stephen Jones Millinery
34 Lexington St.,
London W1

Rainwear:

Burberrys Limited
18 The Haymarket,
London SW1

CANADIAN SOURCES

Department Stores

The Bay
Bloor & East,
Toronto, ONT M4W 3H7

Eatons
290 Young St.,
Toronto, ONT M5B 1C8

Simpsons
176 Young St.,
Toronto, ONT M5C 2L7

General Accessories

Holt Renfrew
50 Bloor St. W.,
Toronto, ONT M4W 1A1

Liptons
Toronto Eaton Centre
1 Dundas St.,
Toronto, ONT M5B 2H1

One + One
Toronto Eaton Centre
1 Dundas St.,
Toronto, ONT M5B 2H1

Your Choice
Toronto Eaton Centre
1 Dundas St.,
Toronto, ONT M5B 2H1

Jewellery

Birks
Toronto Eaton Centre
1 Dundas St.,
Toronto, ONT M5B 2H1

Yu
Toronto Eaton Centre
1 Dundas St.,
Toronto, ONT M5B 1C8

Shoes

Calderone Shoes
Yorkdale Shopping Centre,
Toronto, ONT M98 3Y8

Scarves

Echo Scarves
111 Peter St.,
Toronto, ONT M5V 2H1

Index:

A

Acupuncture, 73
Allergies, to metals, pierced ears and, 69
All-in-one (undergarment), 42, 47
Amber, 54
Amethyst, 54
Ankle socks, 37, 38
Aquamarine, 54
Autumn wear, 10–12
   gloves, 125
   hats, 91–94
Aviator glasses, 20

B

Bags. *See* Handbags; Shoulder bags
Bandeaus, 40
Basic wardrobe, 8–15
Beach wear, 13
Bed jacket, 45
Belts, 113–18
   high heels and, for semiformal evening occasions, 136
Bennis, Susan, 85
Berenson, Marisa, 69
Berets, 91
Bertie (shoe brand), 75
Black dresses, 14
   legwear to complement, 36
Black-tie affairs, 140
Blass, Bill, 101
Blazers
   for semiformal daytime wear, 135
   for work, 11, 13
Blouses
   for leisure wear, 12
   for work, 10–11
Body figure, belts and, 118
Bodyhose, 49
Bodywear, high-tech, 49
Boot liners, 35, 36
Boots, 77
   outfits coordinated with, 86
   purchase considerations for, 85
   weather and, 87
Bows, 100
Bracelets, 52, 69–71
Bras, 40–41
   silk blouses and, 29
Bra-slips, 46
Brass, 56
   necklaces, 62
Breasts, bra size and, 40
Briefcases, 108–10
British Museum (London), 58
Bronze, 56, 64
Bryant, Russell, 105
Business trips, 133–34

C

Camisoles, 42, 43, 44
Canvas shoulder bags, 105
Capezio, 49
Cartier (jeweller), 59
Carushka, 49
Casio, 59–60
Chains for eyeglasses, 27
Cinnabar, 54, 70
Citrine, 54
Claiborne, Liz, 108
Clarks (shoe company), 87
Clasps for pearls, 53
Cloches, 93–94
Clothing dyes, 39
Clothing material
   exercise and, 13, 34
   hang of, undergarments and, 29
Clutches, 110–11
Coats, winter, for work, 11
Contact lenses, 26–27
   See also Eyeglasses; Sunglasses
Copper, 56, 64
Coral, 54, 63, 64, 70
Cotton
   as natural fiber, 34
   shoulder bags, 106–7
   socks, dyeing and inking of, 39
Cowls, 96
Crocodile skin
   clutches, 111
   shoes, 78, 81
Crystal, 54, 56–58, 64
Cuff links, 71
Cuffs, bracelets and, 52.
   brass, 62

D

Dance tights, 35
Danish Schoolbag, 107
Danskin, 49
Denim, 12
Diamonds, 54
Dior, Christian, 38, 56
Dresses
   black. *See* Black dresses
   essential lingerie with, 46
   for formal affairs, 140
   kimonos as, 45
   legwear to complement, 36
   for semiformal daytime wear, 135
   silk, for semiformal evening occasions, 136
   socks with, 38
   for work, 12
Dressing gowns, vintage, 45
Dyes, 39

E

Earrings, 64–65
   eyeglass selection and, 20
   pierced vs. clip-on, 67–69
Ears, accessories for, 66
Ebony, 54
Edwards, Warren, 85
Embroidery of socks, 39
Emeralds, 54
Espadrilles, 78
Evening wear
   basic wardrobe for, 14–15
   belts for, 115–17
   bracelets for, 69, 70
   gloves for, 126
   handbags for, 110–11
   legwear for, 36
   scarves for, 123–24
   for semiformal occasions, 136
   shoes for, 78
Exercise
   bodywear for, 49
   bra for, 40
   natural fibers and, 13, 34
   tights for, 34, 35
Eye colour, gemstones and, 54
Eyeglasses
   care of, 22
   chains for, 27
   frames for, 18–22
   lenses for, 18
   See also Contact lenses; Sunglasses
Eyewear. *See* Contact lenses; Eyeglasses; Sunglasses

F

Facial features
   earrings and, 64
   eyeglass frames and, 18, 21–22
   hat selection and, 90–91
   velvet head wrap and, 100
Fedoras, 91–92
Feet
   as body nerve centers, 73
   shoes and appearance of, 77
Ferragamo (shoe brand), 75
Figure, belts and, 118
Fiorucci, 87
Fishnet pantyhose, 31, 82
Flexitard, 49
Formal wear, 140–41
Fox, Peter, 85
Fringe on socks, 39

G

Garter belts, 33
Gauntlets, 124–27
Gemstones, 54, 64, 69
Givenchy, Hubert de, 101
Glasses. *See* Contact lenses; Eyeglasses; Sunglasses
Gloves, 113, 124–127
   socks to accentuate, 38
Gold
   bracelets, 70, 71
   care of, 55
   earrings, 64, 69
   necklaces, 61–62
   substitutes for, 56
   wearing of, 55
Gucci, 85, 104

H

Hair, ornaments for, 71
Hair colour
   eyeglass frames and, 22
   gemstones and, 54
Handbags
   for evening wear, 110–11
   wardrobe and, 103
   See also Shoulder bags
Harrod's, 107
Hats
   for autumn and winter, 91–94
   dress, 93–94
   facial feature in selection of, 90–91
   outfit coordination with, 91
   social importance of, 89
   socks to accentuate, 38
   for spring and summer, 94
   storage of, 95
   as valuable accessories, 90
Head, bows on, 100

Index • 155

Head scarves, 96
Head size, hat selection and, 90–91
Head wraps, 96, 122–123
Hematite, 54
High heels
  belts and, for semiformal evening occasions, 136
  boots, 86–87
  comfort in, 75
  outfit coordination and, 78
  skirt length and, 36
  stiletto, 83
Home, dressing up at, 142
Horn-rimmed glasses, 19–20
Hose, knee-high, 38

I

Ilene Kaufman Designs, 56
Image, eyeglass styles and, 19
Ivory, 54, 64

J

Jade, 54, 64, 70
Jeans
  for leisure wear, 12
  socks with, 38
Jewellery
  functionality of, 51
  materials for, 52–59
  period, 52, 58
  style mixing of, 52
  See also specific articles of jewellery
Job interviews, 130
Johnson, Betsey, 51
Jourdan, Charles, 75, 85
Jumpers
  for leisure wear, 12
  for work, 11
Jumpsuits, 13

K

Kamali, Norma, 38
Keaton, Diane, 19
Kimonos, 45
Klein, Calvin, 101
Knee-high hose, 38
Knit caps, 96

L

Lace
  leg size and, 36
  as pantyhose, 31, 32, 36
Lama, Tony, 86
Lapis lazuli, 54
Le Sportsac (shoulder bag), 106
Leather, care of, 81
Lee, Jeanette, 24
Leggings, 35
Legs
  pantyhose and appearance of, 30–31, 36
  shoes and appearance of, 77
Legwear. *See specific types of legwear*
Leisure wear, 12, 13
  belts for, 115
  bracelets for, 69, 70
  shoes for, 78, 79
Leotards, 13, 49
Light, eyeglasses and, 18, 23
Lingerie
  definition of, 29
  See also specific articles of lingerie
Lizard skin
  handbags, 111
  shoes, 78, 81
  watch bands, 59
Loafers, 78
London Fog, 100
Long johns, 35, 36
Loren, Sophia, 17
Lorgnettes, 27

M

MacLaine, Shirley, 69
Macy's, 104
Metals, allergies to, pierced ears and, 69
Metropolitan Museum of Art (New York), 51, 58
Mills, Donna, 48
Minaudières, 111
Miss Selfridge's (store), 104
Mittens, 124–27
Monograms on briefcases, 110
Mother-of-pearl, 54, 64, 70
Museum of Modern Art (New York), 60

N

Natural fibers, 13, 34
Necklaces
  earrings coordinated with, 64
  eyeglass selection and, 20
  garment neckline and, 52
  gold, 61–62
  pearl, 60–61
  plastic, 63
  rhinestone, 63
  silver, 63
Neckties, scarves as, 121

O

Office parties, 132–33
Olga's Christina No Bounce Sportsbra, 40
Onyx, 54, 64
Opal, 54

P

Paisley, as scarf pattern, 96, 120, 123
Pants
  kimonos with, 45
  knee-high hose under, 38
  knit, 13
  for semiformal daytime wear, 134–35
  socks with, 38
  for work, 10, 13
Pantsuits
  pantyhose with, 36
  for work, 10
Pantyhose
  basics of, 30–31
  care of, 33
  checklist of, 32
  matching clothing with, 36
  purchasing of, 32
Pearls, 53, 60–61, 64, 69, 70
Pendants, 63
Peridot, 54
Period jewellery, 52, 58
Physical exertion, natural fibers and, 13, 34
Pierced ears, 67–69
Pillbox hats, 93, 94
Plastic
  eyeglass lenses, 18
  jewellery, 58–59
  necklaces, 63
  watches, 60
Pocket squares, 123
Precious gemstones, 54, 64, 69
Purses. *See* Handbags
Pyjamas, 35, 45

Q

Quant, Mary, 38
Quartz, 54, 64
Quick changes, 145

R

Rain hats, 93
Raincoats, for work, 11
Rhinestones
  bracelets, 70
  earrings, 64
  as jewellery, 58
  necklaces, 63
  on pantyhose, 30, 31
Rings, 51
Robes, vintage, 45
Rubies, 54
Rubino, Beth, 145
Running shoes, 77

S

Sacha (shoe brand), 75
Saks, Jane, 90
Sandals, 79
Sapphire, 54
Sarongs, 123
Sashes, 118
Satin
  belts, 117
  purses, 111
Scarves, 113
  evening, 123–24
  head, 96
  socks to accentuate, 38
  styling of, 118–23
Schutz, Biba, 63
Seasons, changing of, wardrobe for, 144
Semiformal dressing, daytime, 134–36
Semiprecious gemstones, 54, 64, 69
Shawls, 96
Shoes
  black as versatile color for, 77
  care of, 81
  comfort of, 74–75
  for evening wear, 78
  for formal affairs, 140
  handbag coordination with, 111
  health and, 73
  high heels. *See* High heels
  leather soles on, 81
  leg and foot appearance and, 77
  legwear to complement, 36
  for leisure wear, 12, 78, 79
  outfit coordination and, 78
  pantyhose wear and, 33
  parts of, 74
  price considerations for, 75
  quality of, 74–77
  for sports, 13, 77
  straps on, 84
  for summer wear, 79
  See also Boots
Shopping strategies, 151
Shorts, 13
  socks with, 38
Shoulder bags, 104–7
Silk
  bra outline and, 29
  camisoles, 42, 43
  dresses, for semiformal evening occasions, 136
  stockings, 33
Silver, 56
  belt buckles, 117
  bracelets, 70, 71
  earrings, 64, 69
  necklaces, 63
Skin tone
  eyeglass frames and, 22
  gemstones and, 54
Skirts
  boots and, 86
  essential lingerie with, 46
  kimonos with, 45
  leggings and, 35
  legwear to complement, 36
  for leisure wear, 12
  sarongs, 123
  for semiformal daytime wear, 135–36
  shoe style and length of, 36
  socks with, 38
  for work, 11, 12
Slips, 44, 46, 47
Snakeskin belts, 116
Sneakers, 77
Socks
  ankle, 37, 38
  designing of, 39
Sodalite, 54
Spectator (shoe), 78
Sports
  basic wardrobe for, 13
  bodywear for, 49
  bra for, 40
  contact lenses for, 26
Spring wear, 12–13
  hats for, 94
  legwear for, 36
  shoes for, 77
Stiletto heels, 83
Stirrups
  shoe style and, 36
  tights with, 35
Stockings, 33

Studded belts, 116–17
Style, significance of, 129
Suede, care of, 81
Suits for work, 12
Summer wear, 12–13
   hats for, 94
   shoes for, 77, 78
Sunglasses, 23–25
   See also Contact lenses; Eyeglasses
Sunlight, glasses and, 18, 23
Support hose, 31, 38
Swatch (watches), 59, 60
Sweaters
   legwear to complement, 36
   for leisure wear, 12
   for work, 13
Sweatsuits, 13
   socks with, 38
Synthetic materials
   exercise and, 13, 34
   undergarments of, 42, 46

T-shirts
   leggings and, 35
   for work, 13

Tank tops, 13
Tap pants, 45, 46
Teddy (undergarment), 42, 43
Texture of pantyhose, 31, 32
Tie-dyeing, 39
Tiger's-eye, 54, 64, 70
Tights, 34, 35, 36
Timex (watch), 59
Tony Bryant Designs, 105
Topaz, 54
Torquoise, 63, 64
Tortoiseshell
   bracelets, 70
   eyeglass frames, 20–21
Tote bags, 107–8
Totes (hat brand), 93
Totes (umbrella), 100
Travel, business, 133–34
Trocadero (jeweller), 60
Tunics, leggings and, 35
Turbans, 96
Tweed, scarves and, 121

Umbrellas, 100–101
Undergarments. *See specific undergarments*

Unitards, 49

Valenti, Keni, 51, 85, 142, 144
Vanderbilt, Gloria, 17
Vintage clothing, 143
   eyeglass styles and, 19
   undergarments, 45
Vinyl bags, 107
von Furstenberg, Diane, 17
Vreeland, Diana, 29
Vuitton, Louis, 104

W

Wardrobe
   basic, 8–15,
   belts, scarves, and gloves in, 113
   for changing seasons, 144
   handbags in, 103
   imbalances in, 10
   legwear in, 36
   shoes in, 77
   vintage clothing in, 143
Watches, 59–60
   bracelets to accompany, 52

Water buffalo briefcases, 108
Weddings, dressing for, 141
Winter wear, 10–12
   gloves, 125
   hats for, 91–94
Wool
   gloves, 126
   leggings, 35, 36
   scarves, 121
Woolf, Virginia, 19
Work
   basic wardrobe for, 10–13
   belts for, 114–15
   bracelets for, 69, 70
   dress for special occasions concerning, 130–34
   eyeglass styles for, 19
   handbags for, 104
   knee-high hose for, 38
   shoes for, 77
Wraps, 96, 118, 122–23
Wristwatches. *See* Watches

Zircon, 54

PHOTO CREDITS

Alison Baxter (designer): 65(L)
Roger Bester: 34, 35
Ron Boszko—for Biba Schutz Designs: 58(T), 63, 65, 68 —for Wendy Gell: 66(L)
Richard Bowditch for Keni Valenti (designer): 88
Tony Cenicola: 119(L)
John Deane: 8, 11, 14, 22, 25, 26, 37(L), 53(T), 57(L), 70, 78, 82(R), 85, 86, 91, 92(inset), 99(B), 102, 105(L), 109, 110, 115, 119(R), 122, 125, 127, 131(all), 132, 133, 137, 138, 147(all), 148
Design Council: 38; Gill Clement: 68(B); Partridge and Co.: 105(R); MIL Designs/Mulberry Co.: 107; Yuki Collection: 108(L); David Japp: 120; Mulberry Co.: 145
Courtesy of Design Gap: Jeremy Weston, Diana James, Shirley Frost, (designers): 57(R); Clarissa Mitchell (designer): 65(TR); Maggie Gray, Mandy Nash, Jane Kennard (designers): 66(R); Louise Slater, Sue Vernon, Maggie Gray (designers): 71
Courtesy of D.I.M.—Rosy, U.S.A.:32
Sandra DosPassos: 53(B)
Susan Duane: 37(R)
J. Henry Fair: 116
Courtesy of Fifty/50: 58(B)

Michael Goldman for Lady Lynne: 42, 44, 46, 47(all);
for Putumayo: 75, 80, 84, 87, 93, 117, 118, 134, 144
Paul B. Goode: 16, 20, 98, 111(R), 112, 121, 124, 126, 139(R), 146
Courtesy of Hammacher Schlemmer: 100
Courtesy of Laura Ashley: 101, 139(L), 143
Judy Lawne: 95, 142
Courtesy of Liz Claiborne: 92, 108(R), 114(L)
Courtesy of L.L. Bean Inc.: 27
Courtesy of Loewe, London: 81, 104
Frank Maresca: 21, 23, 24, 28, 30, 31, 33, 40, 41, 43, 45, 50, 52, 54, 55, 64, 67, 72, 74, 76, 82(L), 83, 97, 99(T), 106, 114(R), 139(T), 140, 141, 145(T)
Jonathan Pite: 12(T), 77
Photo Trends, P. Kredenser/Shooting Star: 48, 49
Barabara Rosen: 15(T)
Tim Street-Porter: 111(L)
Courtesy of Swatch, U.S.A.: 59
Courtesy of Trifari: 10, 13, 15(L, BR), 61, 62, 90, 94, 128, 135, 136
Courtesy of Western Maine Weavers: 123

Special photography by John Deane
Art direction by Rod Gonzalez
Production by Susan M. Duane
Styling by Michelle Lerner
Hair Styling by Mitsuno Yokoo
Modeling by Carol Dluglos, and Rosemarie of Petite Model Management
Photographic assistance by Larry Chan

Jewellery exclusively by Trifari
Knitwear and gloves exclusively by Aris
Glasses exclusively by Colors In Optics
Rainwear exclusively by Marks Remarks, design by Robert McBride
Bags exclusively by Tony Bryant Designs
Stockings by Splash
Wardrobe by Chaus
Other accessories by L. L. Bean

With special thanks for their cooperation to: Frank Maresca, Michael Goldman, and Paul B. Goode for their photographic contributions; Shari Hymowitz at Trifari, Pat Roscio at Liz Claiborne, Russell Bryant at Tony Bryant Designs, Jane Geelhoed at L.L. Bean, and Suzanne Gibbs at Chaus; Andrea West, Eileen Lerner, Bill Klodie, Kenneth Goldstein, and Robert McBride for accessory design; and to Sylvia Katz for help with photographic research.